COHORT PROGRAMMING AND LEARNING

Improving Educational Experiences for
Adult Learners

The Professional Practices in Adult Education and Human Resource Development Series explores issues and concerns of practitioners who work in the broad range of settings in adult and continuing education and human resource development.

The books are intended to provide information and strategies on how to make practice more effective for professionals and those they serve. They are written from a practical viewpoint and provide a forum for instructors, administrators, policy makers, counselors, trainers, managers, program and organizational developers, instructional designers, and other related professionals.

Michael W. Galbraith
Editor-in-Chief

COHORT PROGRAMMING AND LEARNING

Improving Educational Experiences for Adult Learners

Iris M. Saltiel
Charline S. Russo

Dear Larry,
To a colleague
and friend who challenges
me, makes me laugh at myself
and brings me to new
Professional
heights.
Fondly,
Charline
11.27.01

KRIEGER PUBLISHING COMPANY
MALABAR, FLORIDA
2001

Original Edition 2001

Printed and Published by
KRIEGER PUBLISHING COMPANY
KRIEGER DRIVE
MALABAR, FLORIDA 32950

Library of Congress Cataloging-In-Publication Data

Saltiel, Iris M.
    Cohort programming and learning : improving educational
experiences for adult learners / Iris M. Saltiel, Charline S.
Russo. — Original ed.
        p.   cm. — (Professional practices in adult education and human
resource development series)
    Includes bibliographical references and index.
    ISBN 1-57524-019-X (hardcover : alk. paper)
    1. Adult education. 2. Adult learning. 3. Cohort analysis. I. Russo,
Charline Smith. II. Title. III. Series.

LC5225.L42 S25 2002
374—dc21   2001033871

10 9 8 7 6 5 4 3 2

CONTENTS

PREFACE

Cohort-based programming provides an instructional delivery system incorporating more active, cooperative, and collaborative learning strategies than more traditional methodologies. Each cohort consists of a group of students who enter a program of studies together and complete a series of common learning experiences over a period of time. The structure respects the self-directed aspect of the adult learner and provides the context in which social support can nurture learning.

Instruction provided to learners in a cohort setting gives a unique learning opportunity that builds trust, empowerment, and support among learners while movement is made toward a shared educational goal. This book was brought into existence because we are seeing more and more colleges and universities attempt to bring revolutionary change in professions through this type of innovative structure. Cohort programs are burgeoning. Programs are developing and this model is being used in every setting for any situation where learning is required. Educators in academe should find this text useful. It is also expected that those outside the academy who are involved in any type of education or training will be able to benefit from the perspectives drawn here.

Certain groups of professionals will find this book helpful. They include faculty, administrators, and students using the cohort model. All those who seek out new or distinct ways to improve and change the face of educational programs for adult learners will find information they can use in this text. The same can be said for other professional training grounds, such as schools of management, law, and medicine that also benefit from this particular model of grouping learners together.

We hope that this text can serve as a resource manual for those seeking assistance in developing cohort-based learning programs. This book was designed as a resource for educators who are creating cohort-based programs for the professionals of the industries they serve. The innovations in curriculum we seek are based in a philosophy of learning as the foundation.

The first two chapters are intended to help you understand cohort programming and learning. In Chapter 1, the concept of cohort programming is introduced and definitions are given. Chapter 2 discusses a model of what constitutes a cohort program. Included in this chapter is a description of the four components: the cohort program design and development, curriculum development, teaching-learning strategies, and the learners.

Chapters 3 through 6 delve into the four components of a cohort program. Chapter 3 focuses on cohort program design and development. The chapter walks the reader through starting a cohort-based program by conducting a needs assessment. The design of a cohort-based program and its evaluation is discussed. Chapter 4 explains curriculum development. The structural framework of programming and courses is reviewed along with the characteristics of courses with cohort programs. Next, Chapter 5 centers on teaching-learning strategies, including characteristics of adult as learners, the teaching-learning environment, and the teaching process itself. The concepts of building the network and creating a culture of support and collaboration as they pertain to a cohort program are reviewed. Chapter 6 looks at the cohort experience from the student perspective. Some of the topics in this chapter include distinguishing attributes of adult learners, motivational factors, and the collaborative group learning experience for students. Also covered in this chapter are services that are designed to serve students better.

Finally, the text deals with the implications of using a cohort model for educational programming. Chapter 7 provides examples of how the cohort model affects the greater society at large, and delves into the institutional perspective affecting cohort programs. Chapter 8 explores the policy implications of this model for future practitioners, faculty, and administrators in adult and continuing education.

We believe that the cohort model creates a powerful learning environment that is supportive of greater goals than earning a particular credential or degree. It is our hope that we have provided you with enough information to create or improve a cohort program. We based a substantial amount of this book on our combined experience in developing programming for adult learners. During the time we have been researching this book, much good research has been published dealing in part on the use of cohorts in higher education. We have tried to incorporate as much of it as possible and to include examples from a variety of institutions. Frankly, many of the examples we provided are based on the experiences of our colleagues and ourselves. It is our hope that you will benefit from reading this book and that the answers you seek are within its covers.

ACKNOWLEDGMENTS

We gratefully recognize Fordham University's Executive Leadership Program in educational administration and Columbia University's Adult Education Guided Independent Study (AEGIS) Program for giving us the cohort experience as students. Being part of a cohort was a magical learning journey in our development as professionals.

Our colleagues in adult higher education throughout the nation responded with marvelous resources each time we said, "Help," and we thank you and recognize this text would not be what it is without your assistance. Our team of reviewers—Jean Fleming, Philip Kaplan, Nancy Pruitt, Melissa Stewart, and Linda Wiesner—read, edited, and gave it the "this makes sense" test before giving us the "I'm learning something" thumbs-up and for this, we thank them.

The gift of time our children and husbands gave us to complete this work is one we cherish because of all the things that didn't get done while we wrote. So, to our children we gave the gift of watching us write and rewrite and rewrite, for they learned that nothing worthwhile comes easy. And for Philip and Robert, we say, "It's your turn."

Finally, we thank Michael Galbraith, our editor, for believing in the value of this work and trusting that good things come to those who wait.

THE AUTHORS

Iris M. Saltiel is an assistant professor in the Educational Leadership Department of the Graduate School of Education at Troy State University in Phenix City, Alabama. In addition to her teaching duties, she also supervises graduate interns and advises students pursuing certification in educational leadership and supervision.

Prior to her appointment at Troy State University, she worked at Synovus Service Corporation in Columbus, Georgia. Before joining Synovus, she served as the director of enrollment services and director of corporate programs at Thomas Edison State College in New Jersey.

Saltiel's career in adult education and training has been quite varied in that she has been involved in the development and implementation of educational programming geared toward all types of adult learners. From her early days as coordinator of a federally funded adult literacy dissemination project to developing corporate-based educational and training programs, she has continued to refine her understanding of the successful elements of educational program development, implementation, and management. Her interest in group processes led her to Fordham University's Executive Leadership Program, a cohort-based program designed for educational leaders. Her fascination with the cohort model grew from her doctoral research, which dealt in part with the collegiate support system for cohort students at Fordham University.

Saltiel maintains an active participation in a variety of networks for educators. She is a member of Kappa Delta Pi, the American Association for Adult and Continuing Education, the American Association for Higher Education, the Association for

Supervision and Curriculum Development, and Phi Delta Kappa. She has presented papers, seminars, and workshops at national conferences and published on experiential learning in the workplace, corporate/collegiate collaborative partnerships, partnerships in learning, how adults with multiple responsibilities pursue formal education, support systems for working adults, and training design and evaluation.

She has served as the Industry/Education Partnership Forum field editor for the American Society for Training & Development's *Performance in Practice*. She is the faculty advisor for Troy State's Rho Phi chapter of Kappa Delta Pi. While completing her Ed.D. degree at Fordham University, she was a research fellow with the Project for the Study of Adult Learning in Chicago, Illinois. Saltiel also holds an M.Ed. from Rutgers University in adult education and a B.S. from Trenton State College in special education.

Charline S. Russo is director of Worldwide Clinical Research and Operations Training, Schering Plough Research Institute in Kenilworth, New Jersey. She is responsible for the continuing professional development of all levels of employees in the clinical research and operations organization as well as international medical departments and designs, develops, delivers, and evaluates training worldwide. She received a B.A. degree in history and psychology and the M.B.A. degree from Rutgers University. She was awarded an M.A. degree and her Ed.D. by Columbia University.

Russo's primary teaching and administrative activities have been in the areas of employee training and development, program design, development and evaluation, and adult teaching and learning. Her current research interests lie in the areas of self-directed learning, competency-based models for workplace learning, and alternative teaching-learning strategies. She focuses her attention on employee education and development in the process-centered organization. She has authored a number of articles and papers on personnel and human resource topics and workplace issues.

Russo is a member of the Society for Human Resource Management, the American Society for Training and Development and is a past chair of Region III, Association for Continuing Higher Education. She currently serves as chair, board of directors, NJ ACE-NET, the national network of women leaders in higher education. She is also a member of the Distance Learning Users' Group, a network of corporate and higher education professionals in distance education and videoconferencing.

Before joining Schering Plough, Russo served on the faculties of several schools and colleges of Rutgers University as well as the College of St. Elizabeth. She has also served as director of continuing and distance education at Rutgers University. Russo has been a member of a cohort-based program at Columbia University (AEGIS Program), has designed and developed a cohort-based program at Bloomfield College, and served as a faculty member in a cohort-based program at the College of St. Elizabeth.

CHAPTER 1

Cohort Programming and Learning

The terms *cohort-based program* and *cohort-based learning* refer to a group of individuals who enter a program at the same time, proceed through all classes and academic program requirements together, and complete the program as a group. The use of a cohort is a particular way of grouping participants together in an educational program, creating a learning environment in which a synergy is present and the effectiveness of learners' efforts is increased. Educators, wanting to take advantage of assisted learning, are adopting this model of educational programming, which is particularly suited to the needs of learners today. The structure of cohort programming promotes the exchange of ideas and critical feedback among students and provides a culture in which learners are expected to support each other's progress. It is designed to create "a more supportive and collegial learning environment where trust, openness, and mutual respect are valued" according to Barnett and Muse (1993, p. 403).

In this chapter, cohort programming is defined and distinguished through its similarities and differences from other educational models. The cohort structure and its essence in the program's framework are also discussed. The second part of the chapter explores the significance of the cohort model, including the development of self-directed, collaborative professionals who are leaders in their fields. The chapter concludes with a discussion of the benefits of the cohort model from the student, instructional, departmental, and institutional perspectives.

COHORT PROGRAMMING

A cohort is a group of learners who proceed along the same educational journey together as a group. In cohort-based programs, students are members of a specific group. The term *cohort* is defined by Reynolds and Hebert (1995) as "a group of learners who begin coursework together and remain together to complete a degree, certificate or series" (p. 35). Barnett and Muse (1993) describe the "cohort group structure as a collegial support system for the improvement of the teaching and learning process" (p. 403). The relationships that develop as a result of the unique membership and mission of the cohort provide for the emergence of "peer consultation, networking, and independence," according to Schmuck (1988). It is the defined membership, common goal, and the structured meetings over time that contribute to the definition and formation of a cohort. The intensity of the facilitated relationships within the group is a fundamental characteristic of cohorts.

Cohort Programs Defined

To understand what a cohort-based program is, it is helpful to contrast it with other efforts seeking to foster group interaction to enhance learning. Accelerated class formats, collaborative learning, learning communities, cooperative learning, and team learning are all types of programs used to foster synergistic learning. There are differences among them but all are used within the context of a cohort-based program.

Cohort-based programming is distinguished from other models of educational programming that rely on the interaction of students by the intensity and exclusivity of the group membership. Student support groups, study groups, and other cooperative and collaborative learning approaches also provide opportunities for students to interact, but they tend to be more limited in scope. Support groups are usually a loose group of individuals with changing membership, which provide the emotional support needed by some students as they pursue educational goals. Study groups often develop as an ancillary support for small groups of students to enhance learning through group discussion and reinforcement. Study groups can be formally set up by the college or university or informally by the students themselves.

Cooperative learning experiences have greater similarity with cohort programs than other types of educational models of instruction. Both teach students to work together to achieve a common goal. Cohort-based programs often feature intensive scheduling, although intensive scheduling is not a defining element of a cohort program. An intensive schedule means classes are offered in 3- to 6-hour modules, on weekends or in weeklong blocks, so that the class meets less frequently, but for longer periods of time. Sharing such an arduous schedule reinforces the cohesive bond of the cohort. Although cooperative learning experiences are usually established as an integral part of the educational programming, they are typically limited to a particular course and to the relationship of a particular class with one instructor.

Collaborative learning approaches seek to structure the relationships of the learners within traditional educational settings (an individual course or project) but differ from cohorts in that their primary purpose is to get students to work with faculty to create knowledge together (Landa & Tarule, 1992).

The cohort structure provides the program framework. It encourages all of these teaching methodologies, as well as any others the faculty choose to use. The structural feature that most distinguishes cohorts from other educational programs is the closed membership and impermeable boundary that defines the cohort and differentiates its members from other students. In universities that offer students the option of being in a cohort, the students in the "regular" doctoral program often refer to cohort students as a distinct group who, although pursuing the same degree designation, are different and distinguishable due to their cohort experience.

For cohort members, it is as though they are members of a specific group where one only interacts with those who are members of the club. They assume that only other members can really understand, relate, and provide assistance in dealing with the tasks at hand. The sense of membership is so strong that the greater educational community in which the cohort exists recognizes and respects the identity and independence of the group. Once acknowledged, these outside sources validate it.

Cohort students share a common fate, fostering a sense of community that is not attainable in typical open entry/open exit educational programs. Cohort-based programs are also different in nature from learning communities or other educational programming designed to foster peer interaction, cohesiveness, and support. Learning communities consist of a variety of approaches for connecting courses around a common theme so that students have opportunities for deeper understanding and integration of the material they are learning, and more interaction with one another and their teachers (Smith, 1993). While the cohort model also encourages learners to develop a much higher level of cohesiveness and stronger supportive atmosphere, its structure is different from these other group-based learning structures.

There are many programs using a cohort-based model in formal educational settings. At the postsecondary level, the cohort model can be found in undergraduate, graduate, and doctoral degree programs, as well as certificate programs. It is primarily being utilized with adult students. In contrast to adolescents and children, adult students have a stronger commitment to learning goals rather than the more diffuse social educational focus of younger people. Other educational programs geared to adults are beginning to use this model for programs including basic skills, high school equivalency and completion programs, and English as a second language.

The cohort model is also used to structure groups in corporate training and education programs to ensure that all participants hold common experiences and philosophies. Companies often want to see a particular group of employees obtain a degree or credential and feel that by using the structure of a cohort group the employees will help one another. When the Synovus family of companies launched their leadership programs in 1998, there was much deliberation over how to group participants. They considered whether to mix gender, ethnicity, and length of time with the company, employees from the different companies, as well as length of time living in the South. All of these variables were used to determine the ideal composition of a cohort group in their leadership programs.

Guided by the principles of their corporate philosophy, Synovus eventually decided to make sure that every group had a mixture of all these factors to best serve the multicultural company they had become. It was believed that creating a microcosm of diversity within the programs of the Leadership Institute would facilitate even deeper relationships among the employees within this family of companies. Like other corporations or nonprofit organizations such as hospital or trade associations, Synovus distributed recruitment materials to employees to promote the educational opportunity provided by this special type of program.

Another attractive feature of cohort programs is that they can begin at any time during a calendar year with as many as 25 participants or as few as 12. Some cohort groups are as small as 8 or as large as 30, while the ideal size is 15 participants.

The selection process for students that will comprise a cohort is another aspect that further defines the cohort model. Faculty, administrative personnel, sometimes even students and alumni join together to select students. The goal of many cohort-based programs is to have diverse groups of students, taking into consideration gender, ethnicity, learning style, amount of professional experience, and the administrative aspiration of the participants (Barnett & Caffarella, 1992). It is believed that membership diversity provides a complementary mix of experience, background, and training that will become a maximum "skill bank" for cohort members.

The final benefit we mention is in regard to retention of students. Anecdotal data about cohort programs says that these programs experience students dropping out less frequently than traditional programs. We attribute this to the highly selective nature of the programs, the focused students who tend to participate in them, and the group dynamics and social support existing within cohort-based programs. Evidently, this model works.

To truly understand why the model works, let's look at how cohort programming originated. The question, "Why is it suddenly popular?" requires an answer.

THE EVOLUTION OF COHORT PROGRAMMING

We believe that the notion and use of cohort-based programs predate their appearance in the literature. Perhaps the most familiar examples of cohort-based educational programs are found in training and education for the professions, such as the armed services, business, and law. Other programs that have traditionally utilized the cohort model include professional medical training, such as dentistry, veterinary medicine, and pharmacology. Consider medical or military training programs where the "basic training" is conducted in clearly defined sequences with trainees who stay together as a group and are insulated from interaction with outside individuals. Most trainees complete their training in the specified time frame with each other. Those who are delayed may complete but they do not become real members of another section unless they repeat the entire sequence of the training program with new trainees. Another long-standing example of cohort-based education is apprenticeship training. Although they do not use the term *cohort*, these training programs fulfill the operational definition of a cohort-based program.

Cohort-based programs are still used within many of the professional schools as a way of grouping students (Yerkes, Basom, Norris & Barnett, 1995). However, much expansion of this model has occurred over the past 50 years. Literature on cohort-based programs in higher education reflects this and draws one to the conclusion that cohorts are not really the new phenomenon many believe them to be. Basom, Yerkes, Norris, and Barnett (1995) reported that there were educational leadership programs using a cohort model in the 1940s. The use of cohorts then began to flourish in academe again in the 1960s (Achilles, 1994). When talk turned to educational reform, cohort-based programs reemerged as the way to structure programs. Although they were critically acclaimed for "encouraging a cooperative and collegial culture," they were viewed as "directly challenging the trend toward rationality, order and control" (Basom et al., 1995, p. 1). The cohort structure was abandoned because the hierarchical structures within most of the corporate and societal environments exuded such strong influence against the collaborative networking structural model found in most cohort programs. In view of all that was occurring in the educational society in the 1960s, it is easy to understand why these early efforts were not sustained.

In the 1980s the model was rediscovered. With many fingers pointed at teachers and administrators, the schools' training educational administrators sought out new ways to prepare school administrators and leaders. The overall educational system was attacked for not producing results in such reports as *A Nation at Risk* by the National Commission on Excellence in Education (1983), and *Preparing America's Workforce* by the Center for Policy Alternatives (1987). Over 20 universities associated with the Danforth Foundation's Preparation Program for School Principals decided to use the cohort structure as part of the initiative to reform educational administration degree programs (Barnett & Muse, 1993; Milstein and Associates, 1993; Yerkes, Basom, Norris, , & Barnett, 1995). The cohort model provided university faculty affiliated with the Danforth program with a favorable way to select students and to deliver a coherent, integrated curriculum (Weise, 1992). Given the success of this program structure, it is no surprise that corporate and business-training programs have decided to revisit the cohort model.

SIGNIFICANCE OF THE COHORT MODEL

The cohort model is being used in programs in educational leadership, adult education, and organizational development.

We wondered why. The answer: "It's all about affecting change." One of the goals of these programs is to develop leaders who can change the organization. Businesses and school systems are primary places where training and education take place. One advantage is the intensive lockstep nature of the educational endeavor, which serves to produce professionals who become self-directed collaborative leaders in their fields.

Most of the cohort programs we looked at have the bringing about of change as one of their goals. For example, according to the catalog, the University of Phoenix states one of its goals as wanting to change the nature of adult higher education. Thomas Edison State College began the development of a distance-based cohort Master of Science in Management Program by forming a blue ribbon panel of industry leaders to ensure the inclusion of industry trends and needs. Part of the magic of executive leadership programs in educational administration is the capitalization of an industry trend where people want to be seen as leaders. In addition, many departmental faculty benchmark their programs with other programs across the nation. The resulting effect in educational administration programs is a national reform.

Business schools are reintroducing the cohort model at the masters' level and are introducing it at the undergraduate level in growing numbers. Rutgers Graduate School of Management recently introduced a new cohort program similar to the ones it used in the 1970s. The new program begins with a weekend Outward Bound experience to develop the team-based learning agenda quickly. Students spend the weekend in the woods of northern New Jersey in survival experiences and reflective activities, returning to the real world as a group. According to Dr. Edward Hollander,

> Team building was built into the first-year program, specifically in three experiential sessions and through the use of teams in many classes. For example, in my first semester accounting course, students were required to analyze an industry, working in teams. The management simulation exercise was carried out in teams (one credit course). A follow-up to industry analysis used the same teams in a one-credit course. Finally, the first year ended with a case competition with the whole class competing

in teams. The building of strong interpersonal connections was integral to the program. (personal communication, June 15, 1998)

We see that indeed the marketplace has changed. There are more colleges who want to serve adult learners today than ever before. Our task is to lighten the student load and to redesign the administrative aspects of the program, so students can focus their energies where they need to be: on academics! While the practice is driving the development of student-friendly policies, all institutions that are serving adult learners or other nontraditional groups should express in their mission statement their commitment to the population. This statement should be represented in the functioning of the organization.

BENEFITS OF THE COHORT MODEL

The educational experience for students, faculty, and administrators changes in significant ways in a cohort-based program. The cohort often becomes a powerful group in a brief period of time. Individual members combine together to act as one while the faculty and administrators become the other force. The cohort develops a group memory. Their history together affects the group process and relationship development with faculty and administrators. This creates a wonderful expression of a group on a journey of educational exploration.

Cohort-based programs often bring a sureness and stability to traditional open enrollment programs for administrators. The cyclical schedule that cohort programs employ encourages a special application with due date, interviews with prospective candidates, and official acceptance dates. While some students are attracted because of the administrative structure, others find the friendship and camaraderie the most valuable asset of these programs. For instance, students at Texas A & M University's Professional Studies Doctorate Program said that the "camaraderie among the group gave them the support and motivation needed to strive and reach for higher expectations" (Bratlien, Genzer, Hoyle, & Oates, 1992, p. 87). Open enrollment programming can exist alongside cohort programs, but have a different administrative structure and the students attracted to a cohort program don't want to make the decisions inherent in open enrollment program. We have found that many of the individuals interested in cohort programs as a way of meeting a credentialing requirement are usually focused on seeking the most expedient way to successful completion of their goal.

From the departmental perspective, cohorts have many advantages, which become apparent, for example, when developing programs, scheduling courses, and giving faculty their preferences regarding classrooms. The potential for increases in graduation rates is enhanced, along with the focused curriculum that has minimal electives. Faculty is presented with an opportunity for creativity in course development, structure and delivery, and increased research opportunities.

The instructional advantages of cohort-based programs include the opportunity for creativity in course design beyond the traditional course-by-course approach. The modular, thematic concept within the cohort program model allows for an integrative curriculum design that brings together subject matter that is typically addressed in several different courses. With the focus on leadership, teams, communication, policy, and library research strategies, faculty can develop exciting courses by combining content from previously unique and distinct courses.

Cohort-based programs provide learners with a comprehensive packaged educational program. Students know which courses they will take and when, along with course requirements and schedules. While they give up the ability to choose courses and the order in which they take them, they gain the security of knowing that they will never be closed out of a required course. They can also plan their workloads, at school as well as work and home, more effectively.

SUMMARY

We have presented the cohort-based program model and defined cohort programming in terms of its comparability with and unique differences from other educational program models. The intact nature of cohort learning groups who are proceeding along the same educational journey contributes to the emergence of peer consultation, networking, and independence which mark cohort programming. The defined membership, common goal, and structured meetings over time contribute to the definition and formation of a cohort, creating an intensity of facilitated relationships.

The major significance of the cohort model is the development of self-directed, collaborative professionals who are leaders in their field and will affect change in their organizations. Organizations are seeking qualified people who can lead change efforts as they move from traditional hierarchical structures to more process-centered organizations. Cohort programs, with their team structures and emphasis on peer interaction, support, and collaboration, are perfectly poised to play a major role in this paradigm shift.

We caution those considering the implementation of a cohort-based program in their organization to consider their organization's commitment to adult learners and nontraditional groups. We encourage you to develop recognition of this commitment in the organization's mission statement and ensure that this commitment is evident in its daily functioning. This process is explored in Chapter 3.

Finally, recognizing there are benefits in cohort-based programs for learners, instructional staff, departments, and institutions, we explore the advantages for each. While the focus of this model is to create and develop change leaders, it can become a change agent within the organization that embraces it. Administrators and faculty experience the power of a defined group of learners who develop a memory and power not seen in traditional courses. This changed relationship for and among the students, administration, and faculty changes the learning experience. Faculty members find that while courses are expected to provide a total educational experience for the students, it gives them a greater opportunity for creativity and collaboration in course design and delivery. It also enhances their networks for research opportunities. Administrators find that the defined schedules required by cohort programs bring greater certainty to their resource planning process. Students, while surrendering the freedom to select classes and schedules, are now guaranteed courses and given the ability to plan their academic work and personal schedules more effectively.

CHAPTER 2

Understanding Cohort Programs

Grouping learners together and calling them a cohort is not a true cohort program. The process is actually quite complex. To truly understand what a cohort-based program is, we need to separate the components and examine each one individually. While we tend to think that this type of program is primarily an administrative structure, it is much more than that. The administrative structure of admitting a group of students into a program who proceed lockstep together until they fulfill graduation requirements is the outer shell, the formal organizational structure. The value and essence of the program are on the inside, for it is the pieces of the model that make it truly marvelous.

In this chapter, we will discuss basic informational needs and critical questions to ask in the decision-making process. This will be done within the framework of the cohort program model, which includes four components: (1) design and development, (2) curriculum development, (3) teaching-learning strategies, and (4) learners.

CRITICAL CONSIDERATIONS IN THE COHORT DECISION PROCESS

At first glance, quality cohort programming can have the appearance of simplicity and clarity. Although the concept appears easy to implement, do not be deceived. The establishment and maintenance of such a learning environment can be a formidable task. Cohort groupings in educational programs are used when aspirations are high, as in programs designed to create business or educational leaders. The goal is to create an environment that is highly structured, trusting, and safe, and, which fosters learning how to trust and work with others against formidable odds. This does not just happen. It takes a lot of work. As in the development of any new program, there is basic information you need to have. Begin by asking the following questions:

- What is the goal of the program?
- What organizational need will be met by the development of this program?
- Who are the critical organizational members and do they support this program model?
- Who are the people that compose the target audience?
- Which organizational area will own the program?

Answers to these questions do not always come easily or quickly. Knowing whom you want to reach and what they need is essential in designing any training or educational program. Timothy Gray Davies (1997) of Colorado State University described the population for his new doctoral program as faculty and professionals from 15 community colleges throughout the Rocky Mountain region. Since physical accessibility is a real issue, "the hub element of the program is the cohort grouping of students" (p. 66). The decision to develop this type of program was made because "the cohort provides the nucleus for work on leadership and teambuilding skills; provides a safe environment in which to risk new behaviors; and provides the positive peer pressure, reinforcement and support critical for successful completion of a doctoral program" (p. 66).

THE MODEL

Developing cohort-based programming requires four components. Design and development is the creative phase that launches the program, incorporating administrative issues and processes as well as program design. In the curriculum development component, the courses and their content are clarified. Next, our attention is focused on teaching-learning strategies as we seek practical ways to improve and enhance practice. Completing this model are the learners who are attracted to this type of educational experience.

Design and Development

The design elements of a cohort-based program provide the foundation for the development and then creation of a new program. This design and development phase is what most people call "starting up." This is where your hopes, dreams, and aspirations for the program are presented for discussion. It is also the time to voice concerns over potential problems before allowing them to develop.

Administrative matters and processes need to be developed that support the goals of the program and will provide the basis for automated student procedures. For example, students shouldn't be expected to register for classes in person during daytime hours if the program is designed for working adults. In this case, course registration can take place as part of a class or via the Internet or fax machine. Always keep in mind who your clientele is and what their needs are when developing administrative or bureaucratic processes. We will review administrative considerations in detail in Chapter 3.

Administrators find that the cohort model provides educational and training programs with a favorable way to select students and to deliver a coherent, structured curriculum. These processes for student selection and course delivery must be grounded in statement of purpose or program philosophy. For example, the philosophy of Regis University's School for Professional Studies and New Ventures states that their programs are designed to meet the needs of experienced, reflective adults who have not had the opportunity for college degrees. Thus, they tend to structure many of the courses in their degree programs as accelerated courses. These fundamental principles guide the ways in which your program will operate.

Most program developers take into consideration group dynamics theory as part of the program design phase. Knowledge about the special qualities that groups possess helps the program developer to understand how members of the cohort group will interact with each other and how critical that interaction is to program success.

Often, one of the goals faculty and staff have is to encourage learners to act as a support system for one another. This support is professional, academic, and often personal. Learners bring the resources from both their formal and informal sources to the cohort experience. When faculty and staff encourage students to share information and to act as a resource to one another, it liberates the students to have the freedom to share. They are on their way to becoming a networked community of learners. In the program design faculty and staff can create initial experiences that require collaboration where students serve as primary resources to each other (like interview a professional in the field, survey adults in educational programs) in order to encourage group processes to work.

Another consideration that should be explored is who holds official and unofficial power. Keep the following questions in the back of your mind as you are designing the program. Answers to these questions will enhance the design and development process as well as create important "shoulders to tap" when the need arises.

- How can senior administrative support for the program be communicated to other departments in the institution?
- Who should be included in program planning?
- Which department owns the process?
- How will this be communicated?
- Who should be informed about program requirements and schedules?
- What informal power sources should be included, and how?
- Who makes the final decision and how is it made?

Curriculum Development

The framework is set in the design phase with the goals and objectives already having been established and descriptions of courses written as part of the design. Curriculum development is coordinated by the program director. Faculty members who teach the subject area conduct the course development.

Courses in cohort-based degree programs are often intended to be offered in a particular sequence, consecutively and progressively. The sequential course offering enables students to use information from one class in the next. The natural and logical progression from one course to another is quite effective in maintaining the focus on essential content. One advantage for program developers and faculty is that learners take courses in the order that was intended. This approach is advantageous to cohort program administrators because it ensures stable scheduling and accurate forecasts of the number of learners per course.

Once the decisions are made regarding the curriculum objectives, it is time to decide the methods, techniques, and devices that will help the program meet its goals. Those on the faculty who have been intimately involved in the development of the cohort program should be given the lead in this area. While you may be an expert in adult education and facilitation of learning, it should be faculty members who decide on appropriate methods, techniques, and devices to be used in course delivery. This process also creates commitment and "buy-in" to the program by the faculty. Recognizing their critical role in the cohort program team enhances the curriculum by ensuring the cohesive and progressive learning of a cohort program experience.

Teaching-Learning Strategies

The strategies employed to enhance the learning process are many and varied. Teaching-learning strategies bring all the curriculum plans to life. Some view the selection of teaching strategies as a science; others see it as an art. Either way, varied teaching techniques are essential to accomplish the goal of improving the educational experience for adult learners. The variety ensures that diverse learning styles are recognized and that all learners are included.

Most cohort-based programs are designed to use group dynamic processes that require reflective opportunities to integrate theory, practice, and thinking. Learners gain much from group and individual time to think about, discuss, and analyze the relationships between theory and practice. Consistent use of reflective exercises in the learning environment will teach students the value of the art of reflective practice.

Learners

Cohort programs attract certain types of students. First, and foremost they want to be part of a group. Courses are taken in a certain order and the learners typically do not have choices in what they will take. These programs appeal to students who plan in advance and want no surprises. They are designed to help students achieve their educational goals by removing administrative hurdles and nurturing collaborative and reflective practice. Therefore, the recruitment information must be absolutely clear and may require an interview or essay where the learner divulges information about personal expectations for being a member of a cohort. Typically faculty members read the essays and are involved in the admissions process. The overall recruitment process for a cohort program must be adapted so prospective students will understand the program. The temptation to highlight the program's faculty or the administrative aspects of a cohort program must not outweigh the unique collaborative core value of the program.

The students who seek out this type of program are looking for a different way to earn their credentials. Many don't want a traditional program. They are seeking a package. The cohort-based program is their package. The course order is predetermined. They will not be locked out of courses. Administration (i.e., registration, payments, security, computer accounts, and so on) is simplified because they are processed as a group, with the program administrator "running the gauntlet" for them.

The process of learning as a member of a group brings about a new level of obligation for learning on the part of the learner. It is an experience unlike previous educational experiences. Members of a learning group must focus their energies on the educational experience, beginning with individual inquiry that is then shared and advanced by the group. This enables them to become a member of a community of learners in their cohort.

As cohort members, learners take on the responsibility for their own learning. They are engaged in formal study, while most have multiple roles in addition to that of student. Yet, because of the unique nature of this type of program, they persevere and wish to be part of a group with the same goal as theirs. The learners are on a journey together to earn a degree or certificate as a result of this endeavor. They need the support of the other learners. Accordingly, the teaching strategies must help the learners to achieve their goals. It is also important to remember that the learners are probably products of traditional educational systems that have emphasized individual learning as defined and controlled by an authority figure. In order to become effective learners in a cohort program, they must unlearn individualism and learn collaboration.

SUMMARY

As a program developer designing a cohort-based program, you need to take into consideration its four distinct components: design and development, curriculum development, the teaching-learning strategies that are used in the program, and the specific learners who will attend the program. These four components were briefly reviewed. The next four chapters will discuss each of the four components in depth and provide specific examples.

CHAPTER 3

Program Design and Development

The design and development of cohort programs begin with the goal of working with a group of individuals to achieve a particular goal. We see this in all cohort-based programs. So, we begin with a picture of what we want to achieve. We need to have measurable performance objectives for our learners to achieve. Just as adult learners begin a degree program with a goal statement of "I want to earn a degree," program development begins by discussing what you want to achieve and what you expect learners will be able to do at the completion of your program.

STARTING UP

So, you want to develop or revamp an educational or training program. You've heard a lot about this model called a cohort. It's popular. It's trendy. Let's begin by briefly reviewing some tenets of the cohort structure.

- The learner's educational experience is improved by being a member of a group.
- The lockstep structure improves the quality and consistency of the program.
- Courses are all linked to each other and assignments are integrated.
- Enrollment patterns can be predicted.
- Courses are scheduled for the duration of the program.

Keep in mind that developing relationships among learners is essential. The design must include a lot of interactive activities.

This is why many corporate and collegiate cohort-based programs begin with a focused time together such as weekend retreat, outdoor survival experience, or a residential minicourse. The first time your cohort members meet should be an intensive group dynamic type of experience. There should be a lot of group discussion because it allows for problem solving, which provides insights into power, freedom, and self-expression which are the underlying foundations of cohort-based programming.

Faculty members need to be involved with admissions, orientation, retreats, off-site meetings, cultural events, parties, and so forth. While these activities can be time consuming, they are important to the building of the cohort *joie de vivre*. Conversations with faculty members at several institutions revealed that initially they had concerns regarding these activities because of the extra time involved, but came to enjoy them and also found them to be wonderful networking opportunities.

Needs Assessment

Is there is a market for your program? You need to conduct a needs assessment to find out. Needs assessment strategies include individual and group interviews, surveys, questionnaires, and focus groups. Some people will even conduct a large-scale study. However, most needs assessments are conducted as modest, informal studies, including interviews with key individuals in organizations, surveys of individuals willing to complete brief questionnaires, and modified focus groups of potential participants. Don't forget to include past program records, anecdotal information from current students, demographic information, and known facts on shifts in student interests. Your local industries should be consulted. Do they have a need that could be met by a program you could offer? What is important here is that you do your homework. Prepare yourself to answer the question, How do you know that there is a market for your program? For example, the University of Phoenix meets with corporate, state, and local officials before it decides to establish a field site. Equip yourself with facts, figures, and dollar amounts.

As part of your needs assessment, create a profile of a successful cohort student. Consider the intellectual and social development of adult students in "regular" programs as a base, then add the characteristics of the successful cohort program participant. Creating such a profile will help to identify potential candidates for the program.

At the same time, review the criteria you use when you are developing a new program or deciding whether to continue an existing program. Is it enrollment numbers? Equivalent credit hours? The income that comes from tuition? Program reputation and impact? Or, is it your faculty reputation and recognition? Serving diverse student groups? Bringing new markets to the institution? Think about these aspects of your new program or new program structure if you are revamping a current program.

Mystery Student Analysis

One of the most effective ways to learn about your current system is to take a walk through the system as a student. We suggest the use of a mystery student who is not known to your organization. We have used the following process quite successfully in our administration of adult programs. Have a friend be your mystery student and call the school for information about your program. Follow the mystery student through the process. Does the potential student encounter roadblocks, challenges, and disincentives? How much perseverance must a potential student have to make it through the system to a seat in the classroom? Would you endure the process? Would a student who is seeking a cohort experience continue to knock through the institutional barriers of your institution? Would this potential student be able to recognize the advantages of your program? We suggest that you talk with your mystery student at each stage of the search process and ask such questions as these:

- When you contacted the school, how long did it take to be connected to the appropriate office? Was the switchboard informative, inviting, welcoming?

- How did you get to the right place? Did the office have sufficient information about the program? Could they answer your questions clearly and in a helpful manner?
- Did you contact the admissions office? Did the information from this office match the program literature? Did it match the information you received from the program office?
- Did you receive materials in a timely manner? Was the packet complete and informative? Do you know what is required to complete your course of study?
- Did the literature indicate with whom you should speak if you have questions? Were the answers complete and correct?
- Describe the admissions process. Include your reaction to the application form.
- What supporting documentation was required? Did you understand why?
- How did you receive the decision on your admittance/nonadmittance to the program? Was the information complete? Were you given options, if necessary?
- If you were admitted to the program, describe the advisement process.
- Was there an advisement packet that was easily understood and still professional?
- Do you understand the requirements of your academic program?
- What was the course registration process like? Were you able to register for the courses using a variety of options? How long did it take to complete this process?
- Were there choices in methods of payment? Was the payment process quick?
- Were you informed about security, library, classroom locations, parking, bookstore, food services, health services, and lounging areas? Was the information accurate? Are the hours that these services are available convenient for you? Are these services available in off hours or other locations?
- Were the people you interacted with on the phone and in the offices pleasant, helpful, and informative?
- If you had it to do over, would you? Why or why not?

- What advice would you give to a potential student about our program?

Based on the responses to these questions, your knowledge of the institution, and other data you have collected about similar populations, you can now design an administrative structure to support and facilitate a cohort-based program.

The mystery student can be a valuable resource for you to learn about your program and institutional systems from a student perspective. We recommend that the mystery student only be used for feedback on your administrative systems and not continue in the program. That is, unless the mystery student, through exploration of your program, has decided to enroll!

Administrative Concerns

The rationale for using the cohort-based program model must be a part of the system you develop. Students select these programs because membership in a group is guaranteed, courses and schedules are lockstep and scheduled in an advance, and there is administrative simplicity when dealing with the institution (e.g., registration, bursar, parking, security). Don't forget to include these components in your design.

Your program needs an administrative home. There are usually two primary options: house the program in your office as a centralized system or decentralize the program so that different offices own aspects. The decision to house the program should be determined by what is in the best interests of the students. Students shouldn't have to deal with procedures and protocols that exist for convenience of staff.

Colleges will often place the program in offices other than those that seem most obvious. Sometimes programs are housed in the academic department that sponsors the program or in the dean's office. Some are even located in adult learning centers. As you decide on the administrative structure for the cohort-based program, ask yourself, "How will this system support the cohort program mission?" Consider if there is anything that might inhibit the support of the cohort program, such as it being the only program on campus on Saturdays. With the bookstore, library, and snack area closed, students will find there are no supports available to them. Can changes be made to the institutional system to support the cohort program?

Remember this systems analysis may expose problems experienced by traditional students. The work involved in this analysis can provide benefits beyond cohort program development and can give you powerful data that can be used effectively beyond the scope of this process. We caution you to be judicious when you use this information.

Advisory Committee

One way to develop an effective administrative structure for the cohort program is to form a cohort program services committee representing all institutional departments required to service the cohort program. Midlevel administrators from admissions, the registrar, the bursar, the dean, security, the bookstore, food service, the academic department, and student affairs can serve as members of this committee. They should meet formally prior to the start of each cohort program to accomplish several objectives. Initially, they can anticipate and identify potential problem areas and agree on alternative solutions. After the beginning of the first cohort, they can meet to review the process, identify new or continuing problem areas, and agree on alternative solutions. People can keep in touch by e-mail during the time between formal meetings. A listserv would be an effective way of keeping everyone informed. A minimal number of goal-directed formal meetings will enhance the potential for this committee's and the cohort program's success.

Think about levels of involvement: Who needs to be involved and when? Consider forming subcommittees within the committee, such as a task force of key players to explore the development of a cohort-based program and the administrative support required. Share the information you collected during your systems analysis with this group. Ask them to consider what you have collected in terms of developing a new system. You might approach this project in the following manner:

- Tell the task force that you are considering a cohort-based program at your institution. As you explain the cohort concept, emphasize that this is an exploratory process and that confidentiality is required. (Be aware that the news will spread anyway.)
- Ask them to review and analyze the reports you accumulated, your experience, and information collected from other sources. Tell them to include their own data in their analysis.
- Invite committee members to a meeting in which you will explore the development of a system that will support and facilitate the cohort program.
- Conduct the meeting, using audiovisual supports, as a "What if?" session. Draft the suggested system, being sure to include red flag areas that impede or stop the flow.
- Write up the notes and drawings, and distribute to task force members, asking them to review the suggested system in terms of feasibility and integrity to the institution. Solicit input from the group on how this program fits within the institution's mission. Ask them for revisions, changes, challenges, and timelines for execution.
- Collect feedback and conduct review as a group, having distributed the feedback prior to the meeting. Develop a system that answers the "Yes, buts" and hesitations or excuses.
- Thank task force members with a personal note, as well as a formal letter copied to their supervisors. (A cohort T-shirt down the road would be lovely!) Also, keep them in the loop as decisions are being made about the program. Invite them to social events with the cohort, since they have invested so much work in its development and their areas are crucial to the program's success.

This procedure will enable you to develop a strong cadre of committee members to champion your goal. You can then design the program with the support of your key members. This group ownership will end up being an essential component to the success of the program.

It is important to include external stakeholders as well as members of your institution in the design of your cohort-based program. Having representatives of the primary industry you intend to serve on your board is essential. You need their voices to inform you of industrywide changes, innovations, and issues. When Thomas Edison State College initially launched their master of science distance-based cohort program with a weekend orientation program, the setting was AT&T's newly opened conference center in Basking Ridge, New Jersey. The kickoff reception and dinner included AT&T VIPs addressing the students about the importance of education and this particular pursuit. The relationship between AT&T and Thomas Edison State College was clearly evident.

DESIGNING A COHORT-BASED PROGRAM

You need a philosophical basis and rationale for using the cohort-based program model. A clearly defined program philosophy will guide your professional practice. Knowing what your mission is and having a clear, defined understanding of your philosophy give you guidance in determining actions to be taken.

For example, Krannert's Executive Master's Program in Management bulletin states that "successful managers must learn throughout their careers." This conviction that learning is a lifelong process is demonstrated throughout all of their programs. They view their prospective clientele as corporate assets who must be nurtured and developed in order to be ready to assume the responsibilities of tomorrow.

The program philosophy you create must be in congruence with the core values and philosophy of your institution. The cohort program should have a clearly defined philosophical statement identifying the basic tenets of the program along with its relationship to the institution and department. For example, the mission statement of Columbia University's Adult Education Guided Independent Study (AEGIS) Program from 1999 states:

> AEGIS is a highly selective, fast-track cohort program leading to the EdD in Adult and Continuing Education for mid-career professionals who work full time, and who choose to pursue a doctorate in a concentrated format. . . . This program is designed for experienced, self-directed professionals capable of completing a rigorous program emphasizing guided independent study.

AEGIS at Columbia is known for its commitment of significant resources to the program. Faculty whom students (called participants) refer to as resource persons endeavor to be seen as peers within the structure of their monthly meetings.

Every academic program has a philosophical basis and rationale. We provide another example for you to consider. National-Louis University's Adult Education Doctoral Program has an average cohort group of 25 students who carry out all of their doctoral work within a "group support and learning model, sharing information and insight, benefiting from continuous collaboration" (NLU Prospectus, p. 3). For NLU, the structure was chosen to provide the opportunity for close collaborative work among a group of peers, all of whom hold extensive work experience and clearly identified needs for formal study.

The nature of the program along with the goals dictates the program structure. Using the cohort model to achieve educational goals should be clearly stated. For instance, one program describes its structure as one in which participants move through the program as one unit. This structured interaction is believed to stimulate creative learning. Once again, the philosophy reflects the importance of peer interaction among a structured group of participants provided by the cohort model.

The Cohort as a Group

A cohort is a type of group. Johnson and Johnson (1987) describe a group as several individuals who are interdependent, while interacting as they hold common attributes and are col-

lectively pursuing shared goals. Groups have "a common boundary agreed upon by all the members of the group" (Luikart,
1977, p. 31). Similarly, Zander (1994) defines groups as, "a set
of persons who interact with and depend on each other—who
collaborate in the activities of their unit and behave in ways that
suit mutual expectations" (p. 9). As members of a cohort, students interact with each other, are interdependent upon one another, are often required to collaborate together on course projects, and hold the shared goal of wanting to complete the
education or training program.

Support

The literature on adult students points to the need for support among students (Cambron-McCabe, Mulkeen, & Wright,
1991; Giles, 1983; Malaney, 1987). Pascarelli and Terenzini
(1991) assert that the college and university environment impacts and affects the students served by it. Recognizing the importance of the informal support that develops among students,
institutions have incorporated support systems as an integral aspect of their educational programs.

Social support theory helps us to understand what individuals gain from the cohort structure designed to support one
another. Maguire (1983) contends social support is "a feeling
and an attitude, as well as an act of concern and compassion,"
provided by friends, good neighbors, and relatives (p. 51). Social
support is based upon an individual's contacts and resources.
These systems are more commonly known as personal support
systems and informal networks. By structuring the learners'
educational experience as a group, we can surmise that colleges
and universities are indeed formalizing the development of a formal support system for learners akin to a support group.

The design of a cohort program creates a system of support
for students, both formal and informal. The system is formal
because it is a part of the institution. Yet, it is still considered
an informal support because it is based upon the informal rela-

tionships among the students. Cohort members assist one another "by acting as a support system and, in the future, cogs in a networking wheel" (Bartz & Calabrese, 1991, p. 148). The underlying assumption is that the cohort members will help each other, empower one another, and be there for each other as future needs arise.

CURRICULUM DESIGN

The goals and objectives of the program along with the course descriptions comprise the curriculum design. Individual course design and methods chosen for course delivery are also considered part of the curriculum. Clear and specific goals are necessary to guide and support program development.

Sources of information to develop the program objectives should include the mission statement, goals and objectives, and planning documents of the institution. In addition, department goals and objectives need to be taken into consideration, along with industry trends and needs. Your program needs a specific mission statement, with goals and objectives that address how the cohort structure assists in meeting programmatic goals. Development of the requirements of the degree program being created should include comparisons with high quality programs at other institutions. Expert faculty and professionals in the field should be consulted.

Typically, the courses that comprise cohort-based degree programs are offered in a particular sequence, consecutively and progressively. The sequential knowledge building process enables students to use information from one class in the next. The natural and logical progression from one course to another clearly marks the progress of the student toward completion and is quite effective in maintaining the focus on essential content. One advantage for program developers and faculty is that learners take courses in the order that was intended. Another benefit is that there is stability to scheduling and accurate forecasts of the number of learners per course can be made.

ADMINISTRATIVE AND INSTITUTIONAL ASPECTS

A strategic planning process provides you with a framework and organized method of exploring the development of a cohort-based program in your institution. Strategic planning gives institutional members and stakeholders an opportunity to participate in decision making, thus making a personal impact on the institution's future.

A critical element of program design is recognizing institutional and individual constraints. This is essential to the realistic and effective implementation and growth of the program. It is better to be familiar with the land mines and roadblocks than to move forward with blinders on. It is also important to identify in advance the demands that the program will place on staff, personally and professionally. Planning up-front will make program development, implementation, and administration more realistic and less prone to failure.

Cohort program placement within the institution is important to the learners as well as administration and faculty. Instructional support for the unique demands of a cohort program begins with being placed in "the right department" with supportive faculty and administration. The cohort is a unique group within a department, which may include other students, but it is a defined identifiable group with specific needs, demands, and focus. Program administrations need to develop an environment that will define the boundaries necessary for the cohort's identity and growth.

Keep in mind that administrators may see a cohort-based program as having certainty and regularity as compared to traditional open enrollment programs because of the cyclical schedule requiring specific application, interview, and acceptance dates. The set policies and procedures required in an effective cohort program provide order and stability to the department where the program is housed. This structure enables the institution to anticipate demands on other areas. Knowing the number of learners and the courses they are taking is a useful predictor of demands on the library, computer center, bookstore, food service, and advisement office as well as the academic department.

Resist the temptation to promise senior administration that you can deliver this new program without any new resources. You will be redeploying resources, and that must be directly stated in your initial conversations with administrative personnel. Also, as the cohort program will impact the institution in other areas (like the library, bursar, admissions, registrar, food service, bookstore, and security), this should be acknowledged. If new resources are necessary, they ought to be mentioned as soon as the need is identified. For example, how will the program director position be funded and staffed? What about support staff, physical space, and resources like computers, software, and additional or dedicated phone lines? We recommend creating a realistic budget, including the number of students required to cover your costs, and sharing it with key players while you are developing support for the program. Finding resources as you develop a program is an effective strategy for obtaining the means to support the program.

One effective way of getting resources is to get a key senior administrator, preferably a finance person, to back the program. The support of this person gives the program credence and strength. Share your thoughts with this person early in the development process, but do not meet without written preparation. Advocacy from the financial area of the institution may give the program credibility at crucial phases in the development and implementation process.

A cohort program focused on serving learners as a group removes individual demands on admissions, the registrar, bursar, and even ancillary services, such as parking. When cohorts are recruited, accepted members of the cohort can have their paperwork, tuition payments, and parking applications processed as a group. Computer systems can code cohort groups for institutional research, as well as for purposes of planning and tracking. The ability to identify the cohorts within an institution enhances the institution's ability to recognize needs more quickly, thus resulting in a more responsive approach to learners' needs. It allows for adjustment opportunities that may be required as well.

Many cohort programs are using their own admission packet along with the standard application information. Information required from students usually includes academic transcripts and training records. To ascertain motivation and assess the students' writing ability, programs are starting to ask students to include a personal written statement on why they want to be in a cohort program. Students will need to access resources such as a library and may even need a computer for on-line access. These types of requirements should be clearly stated in the admissions information. In addition, personal and professional reference letters speaking to the applicant's goals and ability to function in a cohort program are also required by many programs today.

Expenses with cohort programs are fixed (faculty and administration salaries, tuition rates) and if enrollment declines, a given cohort might not be cost effective. However, administrators need to take a long-term perspective, recognizing that with several cohorts in a department, the total number of students will minimize this potential negative impact.

Another likely drawback of cohort-based programs is the "elephant through the snake" effect they can create within the institution (Russo, 1996). The large group of learners who are moving through the institution in lockstep fashion can create a bottleneck for support departments as well as the responsible academic unit. Individual departments may experience stress from the heightened demand of serving a whole group at the same time as opposed to serving individual students.

The cohort program course schedule can be used as a predictor of service demands for specific departments. Effective planning and coordination between departments are required. This intensifies the need for organizational communication and cooperation. This need for intraorganizational collaboration demands effective and efficient mid- and senior-level administrators. Informal networks and ad hoc arrangements will not enable departments to conduct serious, long-term cohort programs.

Potential disadvantages include the possibility of a small cohort group and the chance that some learners may miss part of the sequence; they "stop out" of the cohort. Keep in the mind the necessity of having policies to govern the program. For example, you need a written policy to address what happens if a student needs to miss a semester or more. Will such students be required to pay a registration or matriculation fee? Will they be allowed to reenroll as a member of their cohort? Do they need to join a new cohort? Is there a time limit? These are all questions to ponder as you consider how to handle a cohort student who has to stop out.

Pricing Strategies

How will you determine tuition and fees for the cohort program? Will the program be conducted on-site? Some colleges will package the program costs separately from the individual course tuition by charging one fee for an organization to sponsor a cohort. A fee for the entire program can be derived from determining the anticipated number of semesters, so those learners can be billed on a separate schedule for a prearranged amount. Many costs are often included in this fee. Since the student group schedules are a surety, you can develop a flat fee tuition rate, promising it for that cohort group's academic program. Consider guaranteeing the cost for one year at a time, or charge tuition based on one year (two to three semesters).

What are the fees for part-time study in your institution? If you see the per course fee as a benchmark and multiply it by the number of courses offered in the cohort per semester, is that adequate? What is your general and administrative overhead? Can you add this to the course fee for a flat fee charge? Work with your fiscal officer to get the "real" costs of a cohort-based program before you recommend a pricing strategy. The income stream is predictable, with clearly defined costs, and offers an opportunity to generate significant income for your institution. Be sure that your department/school's share is clearly defined and earmarked. We recommend that this very "sticky wicket" be clearly delineated BEFORE you undertake the formal development and implementation process.

As you determine your fee structure, look at your terminology. If you intend to recruit primarily from the corporate sector, check their tuition aid policies. Corporate tuition aid policies can be very fickle. Make sure that their policies will reimburse the type of fees you will be charging. If your institution charges a tuition enrollment fee that encompasses tuition and other fees, but local corporations will only reimburse employees "per course tuition," your fee structure or terminology may warrant changing.

FACULTY CONSIDERATIONS

One way to gain departmental participation is to offer a portion of the tuition funds to departments as an incentive to participate in the delivery of a cohort-based program. A set percentage of the income, distributed to involved departments, would encourage their support and serve as recognition of the additional workload created by the cohort program. When determining the percentage, take into account typical overload rates, departmental needs, and the long-range implications of such financial incentives.

Asking for faculty volunteers to teach the first cohort is one way to avoid this problem and develop an enthusiastic team. Some programs have offered perks to the faculty in the first year, such as 1 1/2 credits for each credit taught, access to data for research, and support for research activities (e.g., graduate student assistance, computer programs), or even additional professional development opportunities compensated by the university.

Some individuals see this change in faculty-student, faculty-faculty, and faculty-administration relationships as a disadvantage. In traditional academic programs, faculty members design courses independently, based on their knowledge of the subject matter and their determination of what the learning outcomes should be. They teach in a manner that is most comfortable to them and may or may not develop a relationship with individual learners. Although faculty typically meets as a department to discuss curriculum, the coordination and team focus in course delivery are not as critical as they are in cohort-based programs. Allowing faculty to volunteer for the first cohort program can minimize the resistance to these changes in relationships. As in any organizational change process, the pioneers lead the way for those who participate.

INSTRUCTIONAL CONSIDERATIONS

Cohort programs are different from traditional programs. They require faculty, administrative, and student considerations that demand an organizational willingness to think and act outside of the box in order to succeed. Issues concerning faculty and administrative overload (cohort work requirements in addition to traditional work requirements) can overburden the very individuals who are critical to the success of the program within the institution. These issues must be considered and recognized in the design of the program as well as its ongoing administration.

Faculty and Administrative Overload

The time commitment to teach in a cohort program can be quite demanding. Since courses within the cohort program are often part of an accelerated schedule, the curriculum needs to be devised accordingly. Individual courses generally require revisions in order to fit within the program's curriculum. Developing and monitoring individual and group projects and meeting with other program faculty and administration can add significantly to workloads that already may be strained. It is important to recognize this challenge and work with faculty to make the cohort program assignment manageable as well as professionally and personally rewarding. Citing advantages mentioned earlier is a good place to begin. Identifying ways to manage other assignments, including reassignments and committing resources, will help to diminish the faculty's sense of being overwhelmed by the cohort program assignment.

One of the "yeah, buts" that we have experienced with institutions who are considering cohort-based programming concerns faculty and administrative overload. An overload is created when faculty and administrators take on the cohort-based program responsibilities in addition to their current work responsibilities or within a system that doesn't recognize the additional demands created by cohort-based programming. Faculty and administrators are still expected to function within the traditional box, dealing with competing demands as well as an extensive increase in workload. As a rule, faculty members are expected to maintain office hours, participate in institutional, school and departmental governance, conduct and publish research as well as prepare and teach classes (traditional and cohort), review assignments, and give effective and timely feedback. In addition, they need to be available to students via phone, fax, e-mail, in person, and snail mail.

An administrator of a successful weekend college program was available to students in her office Friday evenings and Saturdays until 5 p.m. during the trimester academic year. When she told her supervisor that she would be taking Mondays off, she was told that "we do not take off on Mondays" because taking a day off during the week was unacceptable. The situation became intolerable when the summer schedule started and the rest of the institution was working a 4-day workweek while the trimester schedule of the program required that the administrator work a 6-day week. This rigid adherence to the "regular" operation of the institution led to the administrator leaving the institution. The program has limped along with four changes in leadership in less than 6 years; growth has been stilted and the faculty is no longer actively seeking appointment to the weekend college faculty.

Unfortunately, everyone knows of tales like this that are created by programs designed to serve working adults because they operate at hours other than the regular functioning hours of the institution. Faculty and administrative overload can doom the program even though the program is making significant contributions to the institution's reputation, financial coffers, and head count. If the "worker bees" are feeling put upon and abused, the fallout will affect the program and doom it to failure. The recognition that the cohort-based program is different (that is why it is so appealing) must be accomplished at the highest levels of the institution. The differences these programs create include commitments and work structures that might be unfamiliar or demanding or require special attention and arrangements. To apply the same ground rules and work standards to administrators and faculty who serve these types of programs is unrealistic and attracts failure.

Student Considerations

Students who participate in a cohort program are adults, with all the responsibilities and demands that adults bring with them when they return to school. Consideration of their need to stop out or withdraw for a semester should be given at this stage. Policies on how students can participate in the program or return to the program should be developed and communicated.

Stop-Outs

Students may need to stop out for a period of time and we recommend having a policy to address this since stop-outs will probably occur at different points in the cohort group's experience. If a student is in the first or second semester, that student should join the new cohort. A first semester stop-out should start the program as if a new student; a second semester stop-out can be invited to join a few social gatherings of the next cohort and join them in the second semester. This could also work for a third semester stop-out but a more formal involvement, perhaps an assigned student to partner with, could work effectively.

Beyond the third semester, much more creative strategies are required. You might want to consider having the student rejoin the group and make up the missed course work through independent study or traditional classes. Remember the student is a member of the group and needs the group. The group also identifies with the student. Students may be able to help you to create an alternative to this student's course gap. However, get the consent of faculty before you involve the cohort group. Let the faculty guide the policy development. Use your institutional policy as a model. While there may be exceptions to every rule, you need to have the rule before it can be broken.

Unanticipated Constraints

Constraints most critical to learners have to do with the environmental factors of parking, books, classroom temperature, and refreshments. On-line programs need to include backup and other ways to communicate quickly. Those institutions that provide computers on loan for the student who has a crash are your competition.

EVALUATING YOUR PROGRAM

Program evaluation is an art form, often praised by adult and continuing educators but seldom implemented beyond simple end of course/program reaction forms. As Brookfield (1982) notes, "We acknowledge the importance of evaluation like we resolve to exercise more regularly. Both activities are significant and necessary but both, for whatever good or bad reasons, are rarely implemented" (p. 95). Since limitations on time, money, staff, and skills are usually cited as reasons for failing to evaluate adult education programs, one effective strategy is to commit your resources to evaluation as part of the program planning and development.

As the evaluation strategy is developed, keep in mind the power sources and decision-makers as well as the program objectives. How will you determine program effectiveness? Number of students? Income? Retention? What impact has the program made on the institution in terms of its reputation? Has it added prestige or money? What organizational relationships have you developed that can help the institution in other areas?

We have experienced some very interesting fallout from our programs, including access to key decision-makers in client organizations who now feel free to contact us when they would like to work with the institution. In one case, contacts made through a thorough evaluation led to the donation of printers to a college's computer lab when a company upgraded from black and white to color printers. Creating benchmarks at the initial phases of program development will give you formative as well as summative evaluations providing both current and historical information.

SUMMARY

The goal of working with a group of individuals to achieve a particular mission drives the design and development of cohort-based programs. This underlying objective forms the philosophical basis of the program, influences the structure and administration of the program, and guides the development, including curriculum design. Program development, including a needs assessment that uses a mystery student analysis of the current system, was presented. The design of a cohort-based program, including the establishment of a philosophical basis for the program, curriculum design, administration, and institutional aspects, was discussed. Faculty, instructional, and student considerations were reviewed in terms of their impacts on cohort programs. The chapter concludes with a review of issues to be considered in cohort program evaluation. Establishing benchmarks during the early developmental phases of the program provides the necessary indicators for formative and summative program evaluation, allowing for continuous examination and improvement of the program.

CHAPTER 4

Curriculum Development

Cohort programs, by their nature, require structured flexibility. Accordingly, the curriculum needs to be congruent with the cohort learning experiences. Merging these elements into the curriculum affects the program's success because cohort programs are made up of defined groups, moving through an educational program in lockstep fashion. Some courses that comprise the program often require collaborative, open, discussion-based flexibility in instruction, a willingness to explore uncharted waters while pursuing lines of inquiry that may not have been defined in the original objectives. Program faculty and administration need to maintain the delicate balance between structural rigidity and programmatic flexibility.

Developing curriculum is like cooking a meal once the menu has been established. The goals, objectives, and course descriptions comprise the design. Now it's time to put the plan into action. You will need to improvise as you go along, just as you might when cooking dinner if you discover the mushrooms went bad. Curriculum development has that same innovative aspect, so leave room for creativity. Clear specific goals and objectives are a necessity to guide this process.

THE PROCESS

It is customary for the courses in cohort-based degree programs to be offered in a particular order. Program staff and faculty determine the sequence. Typically courses are offered consecutively and progressively. The program design enables students to utilize knowledge gained from one class in another. A good curriculum is one in which the sequence and content of courses provide the basis for an integrated learning experience within the student and an interactive learning experience with the cohort. Students progress naturally from one course to the next in the way the program was designed. The interplay between the course content and the dynamics within the cohort and between the cohort and the faculty provides an enriching experience that will build and develop as the cohort progresses through the program. Faculty members know how many learners will be in their classes and more importantly who they are. Similarly, the students will develop knowledge of the faculty that is not typical of the usual student-faculty relationship.

Who develops the curriculum is usually dependent on the overall context of the learning program. In academe, faculty members develop the course curriculum. In corporations, subject matter experts (SMEs) develop the course curriculum. Both are considered experts in their areas and knowledgeable in the subject matter to be instructed. Regardless of who develops the course, they must recognize the varied ways people learn as an integral component to the curriculum development process.

Being attuned to the specific structure of the program is as essential in developing the curriculum as is the specific student population to be served. Additionally, appreciating the intrinsic factors of the specific cohort program that influence how people learn within the curriculum design is important because we need to make the adjustments necessary to facilitate learning. People learn in different ways, and the learning that occurs within a cohort is also influenced by the various learning styles of the students. The cohort design is a particular system and so the curriculum design must include support for and accommodation to the needs of the adult learner within the way instruction is structured.

In considering the needs and characteristics of adult learners, we look to Darkenwald and Merriam's principles of learning for guidance. Darkenwald and Merriam (1982) identified eight principles of learning that serve as guidelines for effective facilitation of adult learning strategies.

1. An adult's readiness to learn depends on the amount of previous learning.

2. An adult's intrinsic motivation produces a pervasive and permanent learning.

3. Positive reinforcement is effective.

4. Material to be learned should be presented in an organized fashion.

5. Learning is enhanced by repetition.

6. Meaningful tasks and material are more fully and easily learned.

7. Active participation in learning improves retention.

8. Environmental factors affect learning.

While briefly stated, these principles encompass important standards to be incorporated into course design. They can be used to shape the way the courses are developed as well as the way faculty instructs learners.

STRUCTURAL FRAMEWORK

Cohort-based programs often are used to support new and developing curriculums, where aspects of a field may still be unknown. The emphasis on modules with focused and integrative courses building upon each other is well suited to the cohort program structure. The varied course schedule required for a modular curriculum also fits well with the cohort program model. Rather than have courses meet for 12–15 weeks, they can be scheduled in shorter cycles, in tandem with each other, creating a foundation that builds blocks of knowledge and skill development. For example, a cohort-based program preparing

teachers to enter the corporate world as trainers might be structured to reflect the corporate environment. Not only would
the time frames of the learning required reflect business cycles
rather than the academic calendar, but the sequence and the content of the learning would build and require an integrative understanding for successful completion of the project of training
a trainer.

The successful beginning of a cohort program will require
the parallel experience of a cohort of faculty. The faculty charged
with the task of agreeing on a curriculum will develop that spirit
of oneness as they come together in agreement on the predetermined sequence of courses. The order of the courses must take
into account which courses are prerequisites, which courses can
be offered simultaneously, and which courses are complementary. Student readings and typical homework assignments are
also factors to consider as some courses require more extensive
readings than others do. By deciding course order ahead of time,
you will be better able to make programmatic curricular decisions.

The creation of a cohort program in a traditional academic
setting will provide for some culture shock among the faculty.
Course sequencing and curriculum time frames will affect faculty teaching schedules. Faculty members are often accustomed
to teaching at a certain time, on a particular day of the week,
and in a particular classroom. The program director or department chair typically controls the scheduling of the cohort courses.
In the past, faculty and chairs negotiated scheduling and course
offerings. Now, the curriculum is predefined along with a set
schedule and faculty members are required to accommodate the
program and student schedule. The best way to address the potential problems is to involve the faculty in program development right from the beginning. If faculty members have some
input into design and development, the likelihood of having
their commitment to the success of the program will be improved. While this advice may appear obvious, our experience
has shown us that programs are often designed without faculty
input. Keep in mind, the program is only as good as the instruc-

tion. Good instruction comes from a faculty who is knowledgeable, invested, and trained in the program.

COURSE CHARACTERISTICS

In traditional educational programs, you are a member of a department, responsible for course content in a fairly independent structure. Once other faculty members have approved your course, you design, develop, deliver, and evaluate it based on your knowledge and expectations of the discipline. Curriculum in cohort programs is designed to be a structured, sequential program of studies. Students take courses as building blocks toward completion of a degree or certificate. Most times, they are not given choices in their major requirements, schedules, or faculty. So, the course you teach has a defined place within the curriculum. Knowing the placement of the course within the program allows courses to be planned based on what has been learned in previous classes. It is similar to prerequisite courses in traditional programs except that there is a sequential, building block nature to cohort programs. The students are building on a foundation (i.e., prerequisite courses) where the building blocks are defined and ordered.

Therefore, the faculty needs to work together to ensure that assignments from different courses come together the way you want them to. If particular faculty members are unwilling to work together on program curriculum, the chair must intervene if the program is to be a cohesive course of study. One effective strategy is to ask faculty to review and revise course materials collectively as a group so that everyone can be part of the decision making. Even so, initially, it may be necessary to work around ornery people rather than attempt to gain their support. Again, in addition to the structure and content of the curriculum being relevant to the course of study, the emphasis in developing a curriculum for a cohort program should be one in which a parallel cohort process emerges among the faculty.

The importance of the evolution of the faculty during the

curriculum development phase of the program cannot be stressed enough. In a cohort-based program, courses are built in a sequential manner and must coordinate with, relate to, and build on the other courses in the program. This requires a relationship between cohort faculty that is reflective of the relationship that you want students in the program to have. This modeling of the cohort relationship for the students is part of the inductive learning that promotes the success of a cohort program. The supportive and collegial environment that values trust, openness, mutual respect in the exchange of ideas, and critical feedback needs also to be there for faculty members. Not only will students know that faculty members are not getting along, but it is nearly impossible to build a program among people who do not respect one another's opinion or get along with each other. Although a difference of opinions is necessary in order to generate enough ideas to shape them into the courses you want, trust and respect must be present as part of the working environment.

Intensive scheduling of classes within a cohort program offers a challenge and an opportunity for faculty to facilitate format changes that may be required for successful courses. Including faculty members in planning the curriculum and thus giving them a sense of collective ownership of the curriculum will build in the flexibility to make adjustments that is necessary during the beginning of any new program. Cohort program classes are often offered in 3- to 8-hour modules on weekends, in a week, over several weeks, or on a monthly or bimonthly basis. While the classes meet less frequently, they meet for extended periods of time. This has implications for course design, delivery, and evaluation. The sequential scheduling also has implications for the development of course content, workloads, assignments, and evaluation methods. Because cohorts often meet at times other than the norm, the faculty person also becomes their point person for course registration or administrative matters. As the faculty person in the classroom will get all the inquiries, the benefit of the faculty knowing the entirety of the curriculum becomes obvious.

One trend in many programs is to incorporate project or

portfolio development as part of the requirements. While topics for projects or capstone experiences are assigned, the work among students and faculty is being done in collaboration. Students should be monitored, guided, and given additional resources to access that will expand their thinking. Many faculty members incorporate e-mail as a primary form of communicating and keeping in touch with students. The design of the curriculum should allow for and promote opportunities for students to access the faculty for guidance and direction.

High Level of Interactivity

Courses in cohort-based programs need to be more interactive than their traditional counterparts. Because the students are together from beginning of the program to the end, they tend to be a more cohesive unit. Dialogue is deeper because after the first class together the students begin to know each other. The students have already formed opinions of their classmates and the views they hold. The course work needs to be structured so that the students' various perspectives facilitate the learning experience. A possible analogy to understand the difference between traditional courses and those that occur within a cohort is to consider the difference between an audience watching a movie together in a darkened theater versus an audience becoming participants in an improvisational theater experience. The course work needs to promote that kind of sharing and creation as part of the entire group's learning.

Faculty can utilize a variety of techniques to provide opportunities for different types of interaction in their courses. Case studies, simulations, and outside research are some techniques that can enrich the classroom experience. Debates and role-plays also provide a means of using information in a different way that is highly interactive. While the subject matter may be the same because the students are members of a cohort, the repertoire of techniques used requires something different than traditional lectures. For remember, "good teaching should be a balance of understanding one's self as a teacher and knowing how to develop learning encounters that are meaningful and useful in the promotion of personal and professional growth," (Galbraith, 1998, p. 4).

Students learn more when they are actively engaged in activities that require a high level of involvement. Consider creating in-class and out-of-class assignments that require collaborating with classmates, where students may even be assigned and graded as members of a team. All of these are ways to incorporate a higher level of interactivity into the classroom.

Utilization of Networks of People

A hallmark feature of cohort programs is their development and utilization of networks of people. Students connect with other students, bringing people they know into the circle of classmates to serve as resources, and faculty members serve as both subject matter experts and resource persons to the students. The beauty is in the way that people interact, helping each other to learn.

There are many ways to initiate the development of this type of networking. One way to get students started is to begin the program by having students discuss areas of interests. From this, they discover common areas and begin to see complementary skills and interests of other students. Students then are encouraged to assist each other and frequently bring resources to one another. As they proceed in their program of study, they build upon their relationship and will likely offer external sources of support as the relationships develop and the sense of camaraderie solidifies. In practice, we often see this support system as, "I know someone you can contact for. . . . " As students call upon friends and colleagues of other students, their network grows. The circle expands and connections between individuals strengthen.

This type of professional helping is more commonly brought about in cohort programs than in any other type of educational program. The feeling that "we're all in this together" binds the group so tightly together that their network acts as a type of safety net protecting them from the outside world. The network brings in a practical application to the theoretical concepts being taught in the classroom.

Practical and Theoretical Orientation

One trend we see today is the integration of practical application to theoretical knowledge taught in the classroom. More and more, students are demanding to utilize what they learn in the classroom today in their workplace tomorrow. Since the students are an intact group, projects and assignments can be broadened to encourage more work-related undertakings that build on the networking aspect of the program. This also allows students to extend the knowledge gained from previous courses into the new subject area.

Keep this in mind when, as a department, you all sit down to develop courses and decide on the ways in which they are delivered. Courses that are scheduled later in the curriculum should build on or dovetail earlier courses. For example, research courses where students are expected to develop proposals must follow statistics courses. Since students are always together during these classes, you can draw on the formal class material as well as their personal experiences within the course. Try to ask the learners to refer to their previous learning, gained through personal and professional experiences, as part of your assignments. This rich and complex learning will give faculty and students the opportunity to explore content at the integrative level of learning. It is a challenging and rewarding experience that demands full participation by faculty as well as the students. Faculty members must have current knowledge of research and practice in the field. Students need to be prepared by completing readings and assignments and critically reflecting on their work.

Faculty members can assess the needs, strengths, and areas of improvement required for individual cohorts this way. Allowing faculty members to make adjustments in the course design for each cohort will maintain academic program consistency. And, finally, don't forget that your courses must relate to the goals of the program. While it sounds like obvious advice, sometimes an overzealous effort to comply with state or national initiatives drives the curriculum with more force than the program mission. It is imperative that when developing courses, let your mission and goals guide the process. Many programs in educational leadership are developed in concert with their respective state departments of education to fulfill a particular need.

SUMMARY

Curriculum development is an important function of the program staff and faculty. The nature of cohort-based programs requires a sequential and lockstep curriculum, offered consecutively and progressively. The students in a cohort program are expected to utilize the knowledge gained in one class in another, progressing naturally from one course to the next.

In this chapter, we discussed curriculum development in cohort programs, distinguishing the critical elements in the process. The structural framework emphasizes modules that are focused and integrative courses that build on each other. This building block approach encourages creativity in course scheduling that is unique to cohort programs.

Also considered were the unique course characteristics in cohort programs. Faculty interaction and collaboration are essential to ensure that assignments from courses come together as planned and required. The supportive and collegial environment created for cohort program students, when modeled by the faculty, enhances the program experience for faculty, students, and staff. This high level of interactivity provides faculty with opportunities to utilize a variety of teaching techniques beyond traditional lectures.

The chapter concludes with a review of the practical and theoretical orientation that must be included in curriculum development. Courses must relate to the goals of the program. Working with a group of individuals to achieve a particular goal should be embedded within the courses to create a dynamic, interwoven curriculum.

CHAPTER 5

Teaching-Learning Strategies

Most cohort programs are designed for adult learners. A brief review of adult learning theory will be useful to inform you about the nature of these particular learners. Next we discuss instructional design, including appropriate methods, techniques, and devices that facilitate adult learning. We will then focus on reflective strategies that integrate theory and practice. The selection and organization of learning experiences, teaching strategies and how to select them, and the role of the learner in cohort-based programs will also be discussed. All this leads to the goal of building the network and a culture of mutual support and collaboration.

DISTINGUISHING CHARACTERISTICS OF ADULT LEARNERS

Two distinguishing characteristics of adult learning most frequently advanced by theorists are the adult's autonomy of direction in the act of learning and the use of personal experience as a learning resource (Brookfield, 1986; Candy, 1991; Cross, 1981; Hiemstra & Sisco, 1990; Knowles, 1980). The classics of adult education literature, including Knowles (1981), Cross (1981), Long (1983), Brookfield (1986), and Mezirow (1990), have identified learning principles concerning adult learners that have significant implications for cohort-based program development. The two most salient principles are that adults continue to learn throughout their lifetimes and that their past experiences help or hinder the learning process. These educators admonish teachers to respect the past experience of learners and to connect learners' experiential base to current situations to create dynamic teaching environments. Their emphasis is on how a positive self-concept contributes to learners becoming more responsive to learning. Additionally, they encourage educators to create environments that reinforce positive self-concepts, are supportive of change, value the status of individuals, and promote significant learning for students. They also recognize that adults are strongly motivated to learn in areas relevant to their current developmental tasks, social roles, life crises, and transition periods.

These researchers suggest that voluntary participation in the learning process tends to create a nonthreatening climate that enhances learning. Interactions with peers provide the regular feedback that further strengthens the learning. Collaborative modes of teaching and learning enhance learner self-concepts resulting in more meaningful and effective learning. Collaboration blends learning for autonomous mastery of life with participation in groups providing the greatest satisfaction for learners. For after all, when knowledge is shared, that is when learning occurs.

IDENTIFICATION OF APPROPRIATE METHODS, TECHNIQUES, AND DEVICES

As we have mentioned, faculty takes the lead, initiative, and responsibility for this area of the program. This is one way to retain the talented faculty you are recruiting. One of the really innovative features to National-Louis University's on-line master of adult education program is how the courses combine asynchronous and synchronous utilization of technology along with courses that address collaborative learning critically and instructional communications. The theoretical and practical applications blend together so perfectly that it is seamless. Students keep one foot in the "this is why it works" frame and the other foot in "this is how to do it."

Course delivery options are exploding today. The ways in

which programs are structured reflect the ways in which we are living our lives. There are on-site weekend programs, traditional one night a week meetings, completely virtual classrooms, and the hodgepodge in-between. We see colleges and universities, even corporate universities, using methods, techniques, and devices distinctly oriented to serve their own clientele. The guiding rule here: know your people and what they want and need. By focusing on the needs of your audience, framed within the context of your organizational structure and mission, you are guaranteed to succeed. It is a surefire way to go.

THE TEACHING-LEARNING ENVIRONMENT

Teaching and working with a cohort program differ from other assignments in several ways. When you agree to teach in a cohort program, you enter a culture in which the exchange of ideas and critical feedback among students are expected and encouraged. Learners are counted upon to support each other's progress. The learning environment is designed to be supportive and collegial. Trust, openness, and mutual respect are valued. The students as members of a cohort have an identity among themselves and within the institution. They have a relationship with each other in which there are also expectations of one other as part of the learning experience. Students share goals, and personal as well as professional networks for information. The cohort-based program model expects learners will develop higher levels of cohesiveness in this strong supportive atmosphere.

What are the implications of this unique learning environment for faculty? First of all, faculty members need to understand the dynamics of the cohort group and the power emanating from it. It is not like walking into a traditional class where individual students might form a small group for that class (sharing notes, perhaps assignments, rides, and breaks). The cohort group expects to collaborate, interact, and fully share resources, information, and emotional support with classmates.

Students in cohort groups respond well to highly interactive classes. Nicknamed "fast-trackers," they are focused on their learning experience. Successful completion keeps them highly motivated toward the end of their degree program. They come to class well prepared with the assigned readings and work projects completed. Knowing this, faculty can plan classes that focus on discussions of materials, refer learners to personal or professional experiences that relate to the subject, critically reflect on and challenge or support the material, and develop issues for further exploration. There is no need to lecture on what should have been read. In fact, a class based on a traditional lecture mode will be doomed to failure in a cohort-based program because the students expect to participate in a collaborative, intensive group learning experience.

Faculty members in cohort programs develop knowledge of the students that they do not often have with students in traditional programs. They often share their knowledge of students with each other as they meet to review program issues and refine curriculum. We advise faculty to be aware of stereotypes if similar themes about students are discussed. Learn about the cohort members as individuals as well as group learners. What are their strengths? What are their challenges? How do these strengths and challenges influence and shape the character of the cohort? How does the cohort influence the individual members?

Whatever your placement in the program, you need to get to know the students and the cohort. We have found that an appropriate experiential exercise in your first class will accomplish multiple goals. These goals include breaking down the boundary between you as a new faculty person to an intact group and getting to know them while they get to know you. Apps (1991) recognizes the unique opportunity first sessions have for getting participants to get to know each other. In this situation, he recommends moving the class to another room for at least one time. This offers a break in the routine, can help renew interest, and can have the faculty member starting in the same place as the students who have been together for several courses. He cautions that the instructor make certain that all members know where the alternative room is and that learners who miss the preceding session be informed of the changed meeting place.

This change is an attempt to renew interest in the process, not build hostility and frustration toward the new instructor! Another strategy to accomplish change at this stage is to assign new study teams. Invite the learners to form their own study groups, but encourage them to include people in their groups who may think differently than they do (Apps, 1991, p. 82).

As another example, one faculty person teaching the fourth course in an accelerated cohort program on organizational change began the first class with an introductory exercise. He asked students to think of the organization as a snack. They were asked to describe their snack to the class; the instructor described his snack first in order to demonstrate this abstract activity and to give the students insight into his personality. This was used as an icebreaker because it gave the instructor insight into the students' personalities and perspectives, while helping the instructor see how the students viewed their organizations. Naturally, the exercise provided a foundation for the subject matter. We like this example because while the instructor needed to get to know the students, asking them to introduce themselves at this stage of the program would be inappropriate and would not reveal the insights such an exercise revealed.

Reflective Strategies That Integrate Theory and Practice

The cohort program model and the learners who are drawn to it necessitate a change in the traditional lecture style of delivery. Faculty members become facilitators within the learning process. They mentor learners and often collaborate with them. As mentors, faculty members assume responsibility for promoting a transactional process of learning, which involves active involvement with a mentee as a collaborative partner in learning (Cohen, 1995, pp. 14–15). Mentors should consider each mentee as a unique adult learner. Cohen (1995) suggests that faculty as mentors must be alert and flexible and prepared to make adjustments for differences in individual maturity and learning style. The mentoring role of faculty is a unique feature of cohort programs that provides a dynamic and flexible relationship between faculty and students. The faculty often meets with the students for coordination and team meetings. In some programs, cohort members are even graded jointly.

As mentioned, the faculty's relationship with students in cohort programs is different from that in a traditional course of study. In the classroom environment, the course presentation is more collaborative and explorative, less "talk and chalk" and more "guide and influence." This change in relationship may be unsettling at first; however, as the course progresses, teachers are more enthusiastic about the opportunity to explore material at this level. Interestingly, many faculty members report having been faced with challenges from students who may not be ready for this relationship change. The students state that they want to hear the teacher's position, perceptions, and insights; they are not interested in hearing their own perspective or that of their colleagues. Teachers, believing that students bring a wealth of experience and knowledge to the classroom, are anxious to hear students' insights, perspectives, and opinions. This is a time to negotiate. One faculty member, faced with this dilemma, agreed to share her position, perspective, and insights as a summarizing process, but required that students participate in the course as a seminar, sharing the same with their colleagues, including her.

Selection and Organization of Learning Experiences

Curriculum in cohort programs is typically sequential. Courses build upon and dovetail one another. The materials and assignments from one course are referenced and used in another. Clearly evidenced in all of the cohort doctoral programs is how carefully the learning experiences are selected and organized to maximize the occurrences for students. Each course helps the students to work toward another aspect of their culminating activities: the dissertation. "Focus on your dissertation and build toward its conclusion" is the ongoing theme of the cohort program. The higher education landscape is littered with the remains of that class known as ABD (all but dissertation). To avoid the ABD syndrome within their programs, most cohort program faculty members structure learning experiences to keep students working toward completion.

Teaching Strategies and How You Select Them

This process can be enriching as well as potentially limiting. As cohort members get to know one another, they become a clique-like group. A familiarity develops which can create a sense of intellectual inbreeding. Students have said that they can finish each other's sentences. Anticipating this potential problem, administrators and faculty should create learning situations, projects, and events that continually expand or reconfigure the cohort group as well as draw on the individual networks students bring to the process. For example, cohort group members can be required to work with someone outside of the group to formulate a project or create a learning situation. This strategy will expand the resource base of the group as well as introduce new ideas and ways of thinking. Faculty and administrators should encourage individual work as well as group work to provide a healthy balance between the individual and the group.

Learning projects are student initiated but collaborative. Standards for doctoral study are interpreted through constructive narrative critiques—a labor intensive curriculum design. Stating these philosophical underpinnings up-front and publicly ensures institutional and departmental recognition and commitment to the features of this cohort program that make it successful.

As a faculty member in a cohort program, you should seize this opportunity to create courses within a focused program of study. For example, if your course is in the first group of courses, it should provide a broad base of information about the field of study including areas of study that will follow. While reading assignments may be focused on specific areas within the broad context, the students are to be encouraged to develop research assignments and paper topics that bridge their practical, experienced-based knowledge with theory and authors they are reading. Early in the class, discussions can focus on the broad landscape of the field. As the course progresses and the perspective is firmly in place, readings, assignments, and activities (group discussions, case studies, experiential exercises) should build on the general and begin to explore the specific. The students will be ready to critically analyze and reflect, not just react from a limited (often personal sphere) basis.

It is important to recognize that you are building a shared memory among the cohort members. The cohort as a group will experience each faculty person's teaching. As a new instructor teaches the cohort, the group adds this encounter to its shared memory bank. Therefore, in the program design, introduce the primary significant faculty early in the program, perhaps with a "come and meet the faculty" coffee hour or wine and cheese reception. Many programs require students to participate in an introductory series of exercises or retreat to give all faculty an opportunity to meet each member of a new cohort.

As you design the program with goals and objectives, remember to put in a way to evaluate and assess program achievements. How do you know your program is making a difference? Is your retention and completion rate different than before? Do you have more applicants? Are they of a different quality than previous students? The big questions to answer are, How do you know the program is having an impact and making a difference? What are the indicators and how are you going to measure them?

Many cohort programs use feedback mechanisms from faculty and students to assess the program, including small group discussions and ongoing evaluations of courses and the overall program, including administration and interaction with the institution. The nature of a cohort program—collaborative, facilitative, communication-intensive—requires a feedback loop that supports this critical core component of the program. While traditional programs tend to use end-of-course evaluations, most cohort programs utilize formative evaluations that allow corrective measures during the course. Students know that their feedback will be used to maintain or improve the course or the program so they give their feedback more earnestly than students who are asked to give feedback at the end of a course or program. The latter students will not benefit from any improvements and tend not to give detailed information.

The cohort-based program encourages faculty to become partners with the students in the learning process. By using group process strategies in course delivery, you can become an effective facilitator of the educational partnership. As the subject matter expert, your students gain an informed perspective as well as skills in critical reflection as they develop their leadership and knowledge within the field.

Some group process strategies that work nicely in cohort-based programs are assignments that must be completed as a team of two to four students. These assignments include active learning/practice exercises, debates, and exercises where students apply theory to practice. Some assignments include students working with each other to critique papers or presentations. These are only a smattering of strategies that can be employed and work well. Have fun experimenting with your class and if something doesn't work well, include the students in an analysis of why it was not effective and try again.

THE TEACHING PROCESS

The teaching process of working with a cohort is different. The cohort is a group of students that doesn't change. One of the attributes of this particular type of group is that the students develop a sense of power that comes from holding shared past experiences. There's a memory and a familiarity among cohort members. This sense of familiarity with each other affects how they work with faculty, very much like joining a close-knit large family for a traditional Thanksgiving holiday when you're a vegetarian. When the power of the group is strong, they can weaken professors, by challenging their authority and knowledge base in such ways that at one institution an instructor was left cowering in a corner. The power of the group is the group using their power.

In the first few courses within a cohort program, the group is forming and developing its identity. The students are individuals who have come together to engage in intensive learning along with one another. After the initial courses, the cohort becomes a defined group with an identity and character all its own. This can create a challenge for a faculty member who is just meeting the group. The individuals have become a group; there may be 16 or 20 students sitting in class but they are a collective of one. They are tight-knit supporters of each other. You are the new person who must be aware of this cohesiveness. How can you enter the group and work effectively with it? There are several strategies that faculty members use in working with cohort groups.

If it is an early course in the curriculum, they create learning experiences, which encourage and facilitate the development of the group. For example, an assignment can require interviews of professionals in the field in order to develop a knowledge base about the profession. You can encourage the students to interview each other. They will get to know each other in an expedited and focused way as well as accomplish a valuable course assignment. This is one area you really want to think through prior to the class.

If the course is second or third phase in the program, initial class meetings are the most critical in your dealing with the group power of the cohort. You are meeting the collective one and you will need to use effective interpersonal strategies to be successful. Some methods that work include meeting the group in an informal setting before your class begins—like during a lunch or break period, a department coffee, or a wine and cheese party—or visiting the class before your class begins (be sure to alert your faculty colleague to your anticipated visit). You can also participate in the interviews, orientations, and special seminars. You can have your faculty colleague introduce you (with or without you present) to the group before your class begins. After your class begins, you should introduce yourself with a brief biographical sketch as well as an explanation of why you wanted to be a part of the cohort group program. Be sure to reference previous and future classes and faculty. The understanding and appreciation you demonstrate concerning the program and the group will be an immense advantage to you as you work with the cohort.

Always remember there is a power within the group when you are teaching. The students' roles and relationships are already established among the group. Be sensitive to the dynamics that are going on until you understand them and know where the students are coming from. Keep in mind that group members will communicate with one another constantly regarding your class. Don't make "deals" with one student unless you are willing to do the same for the rest of the class. We're not trying to scare you—just be aware of "the power of the cohort."

Recognize there is a power of the group within the cohort, even when the students don't. It is a given, just like you are the instructor. The students communicate with one another regarding everything all the time. There is a subtle shift in who holds the power. The group dynamics are already established because the cohort members know that they have the power of the collective group. Having painted such a nasty picture, keep in mind the following: the worst-case scenario is portrayed to remind you this is different than teaching a traditional class!

Assignments

The cohort-based program encourages relationships among the students in which they freely share resources, information, and professional networks. The exchange of ideas is an ongoing fluid process. The in-class use of group process strategies for learning becomes vital to the program. Out-of-class assignments such as research topics and papers illustrate the very nature of the cohort program that blurs the definition of independent work. What is "independent" work in a cohort program? Is it individual, not dependent on or affiliated with the work of other students? Is it free from the influence, guidance, or control of the other students? Given the culture created by the supportive and collegial nature of the cohort, the trust and openness that is nurtured and valued, can it be that independent work in the traditional sense is impossible?

What are the implications for faculty in terms of developing assignments as well as ensuring academic integrity? The out-of-class assignments can be individual papers that reflect the use of multiple resources (e.g., library, on-line, human) including colleagues in class. Group projects can be assigned; shared learning experiences can be obligatory. Students can be required to develop projects that include their cohort colleagues. This is particularly valuable in courses that are scheduled early in the curriculum because it fosters team building and group development through resource identification, analysis, and sharing.

Learning contracts have been used with success in many cohort programs. Contracts include course requirements; purpose; objectives; a schedule, including due dates for readings and assignments; and evaluation methods. Included in the learning contract could be a requirement that students define their projects, including purpose, objectives, and expected outcomes, as well as resources to be used. The instructor must approve the student's learning contract for the course.

Adults are learners who need to be active and integrate new information into what they already know. They have met life's challenges by using the skills they will need to succeed in their academic program. However, the connection between the action learning model they have been using and its use and value in the academic world has to be developed by the program administrators and faculty. The cohort-based program environment, with its emphasis on group and action learning strategies, is a perfect environment for the merging of worlds.

Course requirements should be structured to connect the worlds of academe and work. The critical point is to make this connection apparent to potential students. As you walk them through the academic requirements, make reference to the same organization, problem-solving, and implementation skills they have been using in their work lives. When the students discuss a research project and their apprehension about it, ask them to talk about a recent personal project they have undertaken. We often hear about family events (e.g., weddings, reunions) and projects (e.g., remodeling, new home purchase, notable occurrences) that require significant research in order to plan and conduct effectively. So, we can easily transfer the model they have used successfully to accomplish their personal objectives into the academic setting. Now, when we discuss a proposed research project and the steps they need to employ (i.e., problem identification, problem statement, literature search, study, evaluation, recommendation, and implications) we relate it to the real-life model and note how similar the steps are. In their personal projects, they may rely more heavily on active learning, seeking out experts (usually someone who has recently undertaken a similar project) who will often refer them to other experts or sources. Many are using Internet search engines such as Yahoo! to research topics of personal interest. So, when you help students make the connection between their personal research projects and an academic research project, the mystery and fear tend to diminish dramatically.

Grades

Although cohort programs are used for different purposes, i.e., credit, noncredit, or corporate training programs, grading policies in credit cohort programming should be considered carefully in program development. There are several different methods of grading, including the following:

- Pass/fail
- Grade tied to group effort
- Grade tied to individual effort, including tests, projects, papers, teamwork, attendance, and participation.

Many graduate programs use pass/fail grading systems based on individual and group assignments. In the AEGIS Program at Columbia, students are introduced to the grading policy via a discussion that includes the need for collaboration, sharing, and discourse that is unencumbered by concerns about individual grades. There is open discussion about the negative impact concern for the highest/best grade has on a willingness to share, collaborate, and fully discuss ideas.

A common concern about pass/fail grading is that the standards will not be as rigorous as grade-based systems. It is important to discuss standards of a pass/fail system with the students in order to avoid such problems. Learning contracts, mutually developed between individual students and faculty clearly state the conditions, requirements, and standards of the academic work for each course. AEGIS has used learning contracts quite effectively to accomplish this objective. AEGIS students can attest to the rigor of the pass/fail system, several having experienced the opportunity to rewrite papers that did not make the grade.

At the undergraduate level, there is more pressure for grades because many students are being considered for graduate programs that require a grade point average (GPA) and class standing. There are some programs that use the pass/fail system at the undergraduate level but most use traditional grading systems. Most have determined that the students' needs for grades for graduate school consideration outweigh the benefits of a pass/fail system. It is also important to remember that undergraduate students tend to be new to the rigors and demands of college level study and formal grading structures help them develop solid standards of credible academic work.

Grades tied to group efforts are used effectively at both the undergraduate and graduate level. This process encourages interpersonal skills, including communication, teamwork, problem solving and decision making, and conflict resolution—all skills that are highly valued in the process-centered work environments of the 21st century. The MBA Program at Rutgers Graduate School of Management uses group projects quite effectively by having students develop and sign contracts with each other, ensuring clarity of roles, responsibilities, and accountability for these projects. As we all know, this is where group projects often fail; the team contract minimizes this possibility.

A grading policy tied to individual efforts is a more traditional strategy and is used quite successfully in cohort programs at both the undergraduate and graduate levels. Typically, faculty develops the evaluation/assessment criteria for successful completion of a course that includes attendance, participation expectations, and descriptions of papers, projects, and team efforts with grading policies. In cohort programs, there appears to be more attention and rigor given to these ground rules than in traditional programs because of the limited and condensed nature of class meetings. Students plan their course work quite effectively with their work and personal requirements and there is minimal opportunity for misunderstanding, given the specificity. The nature of the cohort program, with its limited time and interwoven classes, does not allow time to make up for misunderstanding and missteps.

Assessing quality is a two-way street. Instructional staff should demonstrate that they are good from the learner's perspective as well. This is in keeping with the philosophy of cohort programming and can be accomplished by several different means. Apps (1991) suggests that a combination of evaluation approaches, including the following:

- Constantly reflecting on your teaching
- Using participant committees to assess teaching in progress
- Using feedback from participants at the end of a course, workshop, or conference (p. 123)

should be used by faculty to assess their teaching.

> "Quality first" or a similar motto must be a part of our teaching, just as it has become a motto for many manufacturers in this country. Adult learners expect quality, they demand it, and they deserve it. (Apps, 1991, p. 125)

The Role of the Learner

Smith (1982) identified six general observations on the nature of learning for adults. Learning is lifelong, is personal, involves change, is partially a function of human development, pertains to experience, and is partially intuitive. Based on these general observations, four essential characteristics of adult learners can be identified. First, the multiple roles and responsibilities of adults result in a different orientation to learning from children and adolescents. Adults want to use the finite time they devote to education effectively; they often take responsibility for identifying what they wish to learn. Second, the many accumulated life experiences of adults result in distinct preferences for learning methods and environments, which often comprise the essentials of individual learning styles. Third, adults pass through a number of developmental phases in the physical, psychological, and social spheres, and the transitions from one phase to another provide for the reinterpretation and rearrangement of past experience. Fourth, adults experience anxiety and ambivalence in their orientation to learning.

There are certain characteristics that generate conditions for learning (Knowles, 1975; Smith, 1982). Adults learn best when they feel the need to learn and when they have a sense of responsibility for what, why and how they learn. Adults use experience as a resource in learning so the learning content and process must be related to a perceived and meaningful relationship to past experience. What is to be learned should be related to the individual's developmental changes and life tasks. The learning method used will foster, to different degrees, the adult's exercise of autonomy. Adults learn more effectively in a non-threatening supportive environment that recognizes different learning styles.

Brookfield (1986) summarizes the work of these researchers by suggesting that throughout their lives, adults learn, with the immediate motives for much of this learning springing from their experiences as they negotiate the transitional stages in the life span. They have diverse learning styles and learn in different ways, at different times, for different purposes. Generally, they prefer their learning activities to be problem centered and to be meaningful to their life situation. Adults want their learning outcomes to have some immediacy of application. Current learning for adults is affected by past experiences that can serve as an enhancement or a hindrance. The adult's self-perception can also affect the learning process. Finally, adults tend to exhibit a tendency toward self-directedness in their learning.

It is this notion of self-directedness that has significant importance to cohort-based programming. Self-directed learning is defined as autonomous learning that is not so much a matter of methodology as of decision making (Knowles, 1983; Long, 1983; Mezirow, 1990). When adults make a conscious and informed choice among learning formats and possible activities on how to best achieve their personal learning goals, they realize the highest level of autonomy. This autonomy is predicated upon decision making arrived at after consideration of all possibilities, based on sufficient knowledge, understanding, and communication skills. Self-directedness is not simply equivalent to learner control over goals and methods of learning, since such control can be exercised without full knowledge of alternative learning goals and possible learning activities. As Chene (1983) noted, autonomy can only be exhibited once the norms and limits of learning activities are known. She states three conditions necessary for learner autonomy: First, an awareness of the process of learning. Second, an appreciation of the norms governing the standards and activities in the area explored. And, finally, learners need the ability to make critical judgments on the basis of this knowledge. Long (1983), using Knowles's andragogical assumptions, defined the self-directedness of adults as a critical consideration in the relationship among teacher, learner, teaching techniques, and content.

The critical point about self-directedness is that it is not a technical process. It is not enough to be in control of goal setting, instructional design, and evaluative procedures. The learner must also be able to judge the worth of learning strategies to achieve a fully adult form of self-directed learning. It is, as Brookfield (1986) notes, an example of efficient bureaucratic functioning. He further explains that self-directed learning is predicated on adults' awareness of their separateness and their consciousness of personal power. "When adults take action to acquire skills and knowledge in order to effect individual and collective interventions, then they are exemplifying the principles of self-directed learning" (p. 58).

Cohort-based programming is built on the notion of effective facilitation of self-directed learners. Adults, as self-directed learners, possess an understanding and awareness of the range of alternative educational programs available to them. Assisting adults to free themselves from externally imposed direction in their learning and encouraging them to become initiators in reshaping their personal, work, political, and recreational lives are central to the role of the cohort-based program director. The more autonomous, informed, and proactive the learners are in a cohort-based program, the greater the probability of their success in the program.

Learners hold an active involvement in the learning process, according to Barnett and Caffarella (1992) when professors primarily act as facilitators instead of traditional lecturers. Acting as a "guide on the side," the faculty member creates learning experiences that draw on the knowledge and experience of the learners, encouraging and guiding the learners as they develop new knowledge. While the role of the facilitator is less of a controlling role for faculty, the skills in effective facilitation are important to the success of this learning process. Facilitation is typically a role that requires faculty to unlearn the lecturer role, the "sage on the stage," and to learn effective group process skills.

Cohort members support each other in ways that traditional learners might not be aware other learners need. For example, when personal or professional issues cause cohort members to consider dropping out of the program, other members support them by encouraging them, assisting them with their work, helping them develop solution-oriented strategies to deal with the problem, or grouping together to protect the member. Many cohort members have referred to help from their fellow students that pulled them through a crisis and kept them in school.

BUILDING THE NETWORK

The cohort-based program experience builds a network of connected students who are learning in a clearly defined group. They develop their own networks, based on knowledge, experience, skills, and resources, within the cohort. As an administrator of a cohort-based program you will want to build the network beyond the cohort experience, build connections for cohorts beyond their student experiences, build connections between other cohort cycles as well as with alumni, and strengthen the connections between cohorts, faculty, program administration, and the institution.

There are several strategies you can use to accomplish successful network building. As we discuss the strategies, think about a spider web. The web has clearly defined structured connectors. It also has delicately designed threads that add to the beauty and intricacy of the web. These threads give the web additional strength, viability, and beauty as well as a sense of connectivity on a total level.

With the picture of the spider web in your mind, picture the formal, organizational structure of the cohort as the clearly defined, structural connectors. The delicately designed threads within the web are the networks created by the students, faculty, and cohort program staff based on knowledge, experience, skills, and resources (including access to external resources beyond the cohort group). Each cohort's network will look and function differently because each cohort group is different. The members of the group will define the web they create, based on their needs, interests, and characters. Just as each spider web is unique, so is each cohort group.

As the cohort program administrator, you are the formal connection between each cohort group as well as their connection to other cohort groups, faculty, alumni, and the institution. How can you maintain the delicate balance of each cohort (much of which is beyond your scope and span of control) yet connect the groups for effective networking beyond the cohort experience? Some successful strategies we recommend include the following:

- Involve cohort members from different groups in orientations and social events as well as formal seminars and panel discussions.
- Ask a cohort alumnus to be a mentor or buddy to a new stu-

dent. The one-on-one connection brings different classes together and strengthens the informal bonding. Mentoring creates a special relationship between the mentor and the mentee.
Through active, empathetic listening, a mentor conveys a
genuine understanding and acceptance of the mentees' feel-
ings; the purpose is to create a psychological climate of trust
which allows mentees (who perceive mentors as listening and
not judging) to honestly share and reflect upon their personal
experiences (positive and negative) as adult learners in education or the workplace (Cohen, 1995, pp. 21–22).

- Schedule research seminars in which cohort members can discuss their research projects with other cohort groups. Post no-
  tices, including research topics, in the cohort class areas and
  lounge. Ask faculty to mention seminars, topics, and date in
  class.
- Review team project topics and invite speakers from other academic institutions, corporations, and other workplace settings (e.g., unions, not-for-profits, professional associations)
  to address these topics from a theoretical as well as a real-
  world perspective. Include alumni, faculty, staff, and administrators from your institution.
- Schedule an event (e.g., picnic, barbecue, dinner), which includes family members and mixed cohort groups, perhaps
  once a year. Include the Adult Student Services Advisory Committee.
- Send motivating communications that include "where we are
  in the school year," cohort member news, and inquiries. Encourage cohort members to submit information and inquiries.
- Offer a continuing education program of relevance to cohort
  groups and alumni. Invite all to the program and include faculty, program staff, and institutional administration. Include
  the Adult Student Services Advisory Committee as well. Build
  in a networking opportunity within the formal program (e.g.,
  breakfast, luncheon, or wine and cheese party at the end).

The essential point to remember here is that you want to
strengthen the webs and enhance the connectivity between
them. This is your base and the inherent strength of the cohort-

based program. Do some brainstorming with students, alumni, and other staff. Ask them for ways to keep them connected, so they learn from each other and see each other as valuable resources.

CREATING A CULTURE OF SUPPORT AND COLLABORATION

The cohort model depends upon a culture in which learners support each other's progress, exchange ideas, and give critical feedback to each other. Members of a cohort group are expected to develop a higher level of cohesiveness and a stronger supportive atmosphere than in traditional academic programs. The strength of the cohort program depends on the individual contributions of the members: students, faculty, and administration. Their interaction is collegial in nature for each recognizes the value the other brings to the experience. Many cohort doctoral programs use a pass-fail grading structure that further supports the collegial nature, not judgmental but academically rigorous and critical. There is recognition that although the faculty brings academic, theoretical rigor to the process, the students bring real-life, active involvement in practice, thus each brings critical elements to a learning environment enriched by both.

In a cohort-based program, it is essential for the faculty to reflect and model the values that the learners are encouraged to portray. This should be supported in the students' experience. Ways for faculty to accomplish this goal are to go through team course development as well as teaching; to frequent program faculty meetings in which courses, students, and other issues are discussed; and to build course requirements and projects or assignments. Not only does this foster the basic values of the cohort program but students are encouraged to interrelate and build their course experiences as a total learning experience instead of isolated, independent classes.

The culture of support and collaboration exemplified by the cohort program is delicate and requires continual attention.

All the members have grown up in the traditional education system and, often without even realizing it, members can slip into formerly learned behaviors. This has implications for students who might become dependent and search for directives, for faculty who might plan a class in a lecture-only mode, and for administrators who might feel that they know best and make decisions without input. It has been our experience that these three traditional modes tend never to happen together. Each member group is keeping the other true to the cohort program philosophy, and the dynamics are often dramatic and exhilarating, which is the nature of collaboration and support.

SUMMARY

Adult learning theory provides valuable insights into the primary participants in cohort programs. We reviewed the role of experience and the fact that adult learners continue to learn throughout their lives focusing on the need for faculty to consider these implications in course development and presentation. Administrators were reminded to create learning environments that reinforce positive self-concepts, are supportive of change, value the status of individuals within a group process, and promote significant learning for students. We reviewed appropriate methods, techniques, and devices to accomplish these objectives. The teaching-learning environment was discussed, including the integration of theory and practice, selection and organization of learning experiences, the teaching process, and the role of the learner. Finally, we described how to build the network and create a culture of support and collaboration.

CHAPTER 6

The Cohort Program Learner

The fulfillment of a lifelong dream—to earn a college degree, professional certification, or a doctorate—is why adults pursue higher education. Many adults in college say that they came to school because they always wanted a college degree, or their parents, grandparents, or spouses always dreamed of their achieving this milestone. They are ready to do something and embark on the adventure of pursuing knowledge through higher education. This chapter focuses on cohort program learners and how to ensure your program is meeting their needs.

CHARACTERISTICS OF LEARNERS

Learners that are attracted to cohort programs share common characteristics. They bring significant "seat of the pants" practical knowledge to the classroom. They are bright, intelligent individuals who are seeking a complete program of study. Potential learners are attracted to the overall package because the selling point is group completion. They want to meet their academic goal and earn a certificate or degree. They are willing to give up course selection in return for a greater certainty of completing the program.

Motivational Factors

Motivational factors that are thought to contribute to an adult entering a college program have been examined by Aslanian and Brickell (1980), Kasworm and Blowers (1994), and many others. In their seminal work on adults and their entry into college, these researchers found that most adults enter college as a result of some change in their lives. The significant changes in life they found were somewhat specific to each gender. Such transitions were found most often to be triggered by family changes for women and career changes for men. These changes in role status are the catalysts for life transitions and the reasons why adults return to school. They need to respond to the changing definitions of their life space and they want the support that a program offering skills, definition, and certification offers. Both factors contribute to their attraction to a cohort-based program. The intellectual stimulation of the academic environment and the quest to fulfill a lifelong dream also motivate all adults seeking further education and training.

How do students shop for the right school or program? Generally, they consider the acquisition of an education serious business. A change in their lives has motivated them to pursue a degree. Changes in the family situation can act as catalysts:

- the empty nest syndrome (children raised, no major focus in life)
- a divorce
- the death of a spouse or other significant person ("Mother always wanted me to get a college degree.")
- the need for job security and more money
- a response to a crisis or the need to cope with it

Changes in employment situations also trigger the pursuit of higher education. Adults will come to your institution because of career needs:

- to remain competitive
- for retraining
- for updating technological skills
- to avoid career obsolescence
- to be interdisciplinary in education as well as job functioning
- for career advancement

This combination of changes in family, employment, or fulfillment of a lifelong dream often results in a serious self-evaluation that brings the adult to the readiness stage. This is when the search for the right school or program begins.

An example of the potential cohort program student was illustrated when we recently began advising a young woman who has a 13-year career with a major pharmaceutical company. She has held several administrative positions, advancing in scope and responsibility with each new position. The creation of a new employee training department in her division combines the possibility of a lifelong dream of teaching with a significant promotion to the next level in the organization. This entry-level management position (more status and an increase in salary) has created the trigger for a life transition for her. She is now researching academic programs and institutions, looking for the best program for her. Like many prospective students, she is shopping for a school. She began her discussion with us by describing her self-assessment that resulted in the recognition of the need for a college degree. She spoke about not wanting to go to school for seven years, not being able to take classes on a traditional schedule, and not being willing to take "lots of irrelevant, uninteresting courses in a haphazard, willy-nilly way." She is a perfect candidate for a cohort program. She has an internal need to achieve and is now driving relentlessly, against what she has always considered to be great odds, toward a program that will facilitate attaining the college degree.

She has concerns about failure and seeks a brighter future. She recognizes that it is better to be propelled by the desire to achieve than handicapped by the fear of failure. Since her academic program will be cosponsored by her employer, she is at first invigorated by the knowledge that they will pay the tuition, books, and fees for her academic program. At the same time, her anxiety level rises. Will the corporate support continue for her to complete the program? Will she be able to perform at the same level as coworkers who are also in the same program? Already, the fear of failure and its potential impact on the work relationship has emerged. In part, that is what is attracting her to a cohort program.

In a cohort program, the course of study is laid out from beginning to end. Students know the order and timeline of their courses from the day they enroll. They don't worry about which course to take or not being able to get into a course. Students know upon acceptance into the program that they will never be blocked from taking a course. The peer support from the other students helps to get them through the program. Students say these programs are designed with success in mind. Cohorts are for students who want more. Typically they want to earn a degree quickly. An accelerated degree program often isn't enough for them. They are serious students, who have finally made the decision to earn a degree. They also recognize that they want to be part of a community of learners. The high value that is placed upon being a member of a community of learners cannot be stressed enough. The successful cohort is comprised of students who are interested in the development of the group process that facilitates learning and therefore completion among all members of their group. They know how to teach and learn from each other and desire the kind of interaction that will lead in their minds to a positive common fate for all.

Collaborative Intensive Group Learning Experience

Although the nature of the collaborative and intensive group learning experience can be very specific to the context of the cohort program, certain features are typical and predictably present in the cohort program learner. All students will likely engage in a similar process as their cohort develops.

Prospective students are often attracted to a cohort-based program because they want to be part of a group who will be learning together. Cohort-based programming promotes the development of relationships among learners to continue in the educational process in several significant ways. Members of the cohort act as a support system for one another, freely sharing resources, information, and emotional support. They share resources such as carpooling, photocopying, or even child care, which strengthens the bonds among group members. In addition to the provision of information and resources, the emotional bonds of the group help individual learners in dealing with group as well as individual stresses. All members benefit from the shared appreciation of each other's academic burdens and can receive support from the group for external stresses like family, occupational, or health problems.

Once a new cohort is formed and the members begin to interact with each other, the bonds begin to develop among the individuals. Their sense of common purpose and problems holds them together. They share information—academic, professional and personal—with each other. When early warning signs of potential difficulty emerge, other cohort members seek the troubled student out and start developing strategies to overcome the problem. The sense of a common fate, the feeling of all being in it together, creates a sense of "if you go, we all go."

Getting to know each other helps the members of the cohort to identify resources within the group. Each cohort group will develop a unique network within the program, consisting of faculty, administrators, and each other, bringing their own individual networks of formal and informal relationships to the cohort. As the group develops and matures, these external resources become part of the network and are shared by other cohort members. Student supporters develop within the group. It is not unusual to see minicohorts develop as study, research, and personal support groups to help the students help themselves.

Part of the cohort development process is the emergence of minicohorts. Minicohorts are small groups within the cohort that form very much like cliques (Saltiel, 1994). Unlike study groups where the learners are assigned to groups by program staff, the students themselves form minicohorts (groups of three to five learners). Minicohorts develop along natural lines of affiliation and are formed by geographical proximity, previous affiliation, ethnicity, age, dissertation topic, or profession. Often minicohorts develop as a result of carpooling, common personal interests, or specific skills and or knowledge that attract cohort members to each other. The attraction is often based upon the desire to access a skill or attribute of another. Proximity provides common core values and complimentary perspectives. Learners in minicohorts seamlessly integrate into the larger cohort. Minicohorts often become coordinating groups within the

larger cohort, bringing interests and specialties together, synthe-
sizing the information and resources while at the same time providing an effective filter for group knowledge and learning.

The support of the cohort group and access to the networks each member has bring strength and increase the odds
for success. For example, in one doctoral cohort group at Columbia University, a minicohort formed within the larger group.
The group roomed together each summer and met for breakfast
before each class meeting. They communicated by phone, voice
mail, and fax between class meetings. They connected on a more
intimate personal level than the group of the whole and knew
just when a group member needed encouragement, coercion, or
a sympathetic ear. This group connected so closely that when
one of them felt overwhelmed by having to do a proposal for
dissertation study and planned to withdraw from the program,
the others banded together and gave support. But it was the con-
tribution of one of the group that got the student through the
crisis. Knowing how real the crisis was, the friend took three
days vacation, came to the student's home, and stayed through
the writing of the first draft. Once that wall was hurdled, the
student was able to continue and finally accomplish a lifelong
dream of earning a doctorate.

Do all cohorts have minicohorts with bonding experiences
like this one? No, of course not, but the students who were
members of the Gang of Five would never have said that they
would have bonded like this, either. Successful business execu-
tives, academics, nurses, and administrators, they left their cor-
porate-business-professional armor at the door and became empowered by the group. We often use this example when we
speak with administrators and faculty about the cohort experience, especially when we speak about the positive powers of students supporting each other.

Each accomplishment builds on the next, creating a chain
of successful completions of steps toward the goal. Learners are
each empowered by the affirmation of their progress and their
membership in the cohort. This contributes to a positive view
of self and further provides reinforcement for continued effort
and completion of the final goals. Students learn that success

through the cohort experience is a powerful motivator and reason to pursue an academic degree via the cohort-based program.

Students Who Are Responsible for Their Own Learning

Students who choose cohort-based programs make a commitment to themselves to be responsible for their own learning. Cohort-based programs are rigorous, challenging, demanding academic experiences designed for those students who are willing to focus and accomplish objectives. Students make a promise to themselves and to other members of the cohort group to have an active involvement in the learning process.

Students see this educational experience as an opportunity to step back, reflect, and learn some different theoretical perspectives regarding life. While considered a luxury by many, this reflective time is necessary for the individual change and development that many cohort leadership programs are striving toward. This critical reflection leads toward group and individual assessment and is essential for personal growth and development.

Cohort group students are often in constant communication with each other, faculty, and administration via e-mail, phone and voice mail, fax and naturally, face-to-face discussions. They connect with each other concerning schoolwork, projects, assignments, and other academic requirements. They also relate on personal and emotional levels using any and all methods of communication available to them. They stay in touch because they know that communication is essential to individual and group success. They also access faculty and administration more regularly, so much so that traditional program students envy and admire their position. It is almost a collegial interaction at this level as well. Faculty and administration are essential elements of the cohort and frequent communication strengthens and enhances the connections among the network.

Cohort learners build on their previous formal and informal learning as well as group learning throughout the program. Because of the predetermined curriculum, students plan together for future learning opportunities in designated courses to come. They work together to develop projects which build over several courses because they know where they are going with their course work and can develop longer-range research themes. In a cohort program, students know each other's assignments, projects, and research topics. They are encouraged to discuss their topics and share information, insights, resources, and perspectives. For example, in most doctoral cohort-based programs, students pass along citations, data, and information about related studies that they discussed while researching their topics to other cohort group students.

Cohort members, by virtue of their roles within the formal group, are often able to develop and deliver joint projects much more effectively than traditional students since they see each other regularly and are expected to collaborate and function as a group. This enriches the learning environment as well as the potential for the final product.

PROGRAMS DESIGNED FOR LEARNERS

In an effort to illustrate cohort program development and how it must necessarily be responsive to the needs of the potential cohort member, we will consider the successful AEGIS Program at Columbia University.

Students in the AEGIS Program at Columbia University often spoke about what attracted them to the doctoral program. Reading the literature, they sensed that this program was designed to meet their learning needs. How? The program was designed for seasoned professionals (5+ years in the field) with a track record of significant professional accomplishments who were seeking an educational experience that drew on that experience while it challenged the learners through rigorous academic study with leaders in the field of adult and continuing education. The program had a clearly defined curriculum and schedule; yet students could define research topics within each major course. In effect within each course the student could develop his or her own line of inquiry and intellectual pursuits while continuing the lockstep schedule. They were expected to define their dissertation topics in the first semester; each subsequent semester, learning contracts were developed (containing course objectives, study projects, and standards of performance) that concluded in a chapter of the dissertation. So while students gave up the freedom to select courses, schedules, and faculty, they gained the certainty of a concentrated focused timetable, academic work that advanced their dissertation study, and the knowledge that they were moving toward their goal.

This notion of giving up and gaining in return is often referred to as "what you lose on the popcorn, you make up on the peanuts." The expression, often used by MBA students in terms of running a business, has relevance for learners in cohort-based programs. While the freedom to select courses, schedules, faculty, and levels of participation (e.g., from actively joining in discussions to passive note taking) is given up, the student gains the certainty of courses, schedule, instructors, teaching-learning environment, and requirements. Emphasizing this popcorn and peanuts effect in your literature and in your discussion with prospective students is valuable. If you can relate the degrees of freedom within the defined courses (e.g., the AEGIS Program model), you will minimize concerns regarding the pursuit of individual academic inquiries.

For adults returning to school, the fear of failure is great. Try to build student experiences on the notion of small wins, with all roads leading to the major accomplishment: the degree. Help students separate the task into manageable pieces and to see each piece, when completed, as a small win. There is a tendency to focus on the big picture, the major achievement. It can feel so overwhelming in its entirety, e.g., "I don't have seven years to go to school." "I can't write a thesis or dissertation." Breaking it up into smaller sections or pieces, then building it back, piece by piece, into the major accomplishment, makes it attainable. As students accomplish each paper, assignment, report and exam; meet each deadline and keep the work schedule on target; contribute to class discussions and have a "right" answer, small wins are accomplished. Just like the blocks of the foundation, sections of courses lead to courses completed which lead to semesters accomplished which lead to degree awarded. Students should be encouraged to chart their academic progress.

Many students keep a copy of their academic degree plan taped to a wall and draw a red line through each milestone as it is reached. It brings the goal of earning a degree one step closer. Many also celebrate each accomplishment. Tell students to reward themselves for each task completed. After all, if they don't say, "I did a good job. Let's celebrate," who will?

In the next section, we explore structural processes that best serve adult learners in cohort-based programs. As this chapter is focused on learners, these processes are viewed from the student vantage point.

Administrative Structure

Students want the ease of one-stop shopping—not a supercenter, but a return to the neighborhood store where the merchant had everything you needed within arms reach. Get the picture? Your administrative structure is your business, not theirs. There are many different ways to structure your processes and the organization.

For example, either the academic department or admissions department can conduct your admissions process. When only faculty selects candidates, admissions representatives are either excluded from the interview and review process or they only have tangential involvement because of the fear that they might be tempted to sell the program to students indiscriminately. Ideally, the admissions department is responsible for marketing and distributing literature for all programs and also establishing the student application folder. The academic department makes the final selection of candidates. Either department can notify applicants that they have been selected for the program.

At Thomas Edison State College in New Jersey, when an applicant is admitted to the college, a letter is immediately computer generated from the admissions director congratulating the person. At the same time, another computer generated letter from the dean of the degree program welcomes the applicant to the program and describes the specific requirements.

You need to outline program requirements and course schedules in your prospectus and all brochures. Prospective students need to see the specific attendance requirements and anticipated graduation date. From the National-Louis University in Illinois bulletin: "The EdD in Adult Education is designed to be completed in three years . . . The dissertation, called a Critical Engagement Project, is integrated throughout the doctoral program." This brochure clearly informs the student of how long the program will take and sets the expectation that the dissertation should be completed within the time frame.

Many programs like their cohort group to number under 25 participants. Larger cohort groups can place demands on the department and institution that cannot be easily accommodated, e.g., faculty, department staff in the library, computer services, bookstore, photocopying, security, food service, and residence halls. The enticement of more tuition can be seductive; however, the strain that a larger cohort can create can diminish the real value of the increased income. If a cohort is small in size (less than 12 participants) there is the potential for negative group dynamics as well as negative economic impact. Many costs are fixed in a cohort program and small group size combined with the factor of attrition can be potentially damaging to the institution. At the outset of the cohort program, a small group size may be necessary to get started. The higher start-up costs can be distributed over larger cohort groups in future programs.

Recruitment

Many schools begin their marketing and recruitment efforts with an announcement in their alumni newsletter or a targeted mailing to a special group of alumni. They want to offer their alumni an opportunity to earn a higher level credential in the same field. Keep in mind, if someone is reading the alumni magazine, that person is connected to the school. Take advantage of this connection. If a potential student contacts you and tells you that information about the program came from an alumnus, send a note or a small thank you token. This show of appreciation tells the alumnus that you recognize the continuing support demonstrated by this connection.

One way to reach this market is to distribute literature that describes the advantages of a cohort-based program. Oftentimes this contact can result in an on-site cohort program. Libraries, religious establishments (churches, synagogues, temples), social organizations, and unions are also good places to display the literature. An advertisement in their newsletters or an announcement is also effective. A church bulletin has a captive audience that will read your announcement while waiting for a service to begin. If you want to use a newspaper ad, the life/leisure and sports sections are the best places to put your ad. You can request that the ad be in the Wednesday life/leisure section and the Sunday and Monday sports sections. These are the most popular sections read by the adult student market.

For graduate degree programs, the workplace is also effective for recruitment. Educational leadership programs can be advertised in schools (K-12), community colleges, and four-year institutions as well as human resource departments of businesses and industries. Hospitals are also a good market for these programs. Advertising in professional journals and participating in professional meetings, "schmoozing" with potential students during meals and breaks, are also effective. Be sure to have business cards and program literature on display. Collect the remaining information after the meeting, or it will be thrown out after you leave.

As you think about your recruitment strategy, remember whom you are attempting to reach . . . busy working adults. Think about your busy life and where information could be made available for you to see in a short space of time. What catches your attention . . . and how? This is a great way to gear your thinking and your strategy in the right direction.

Personal connections are the foundation of cohort-based programs. Another recruitment tactic: hold an open house at the school. Use the same advertisement strategy described above and invite potential students to come and learn how they can complete their degree while working and maintaining personal responsibilities.

This approach was used to announce a new weekend college, cohort-based program at a college in New Jersey. Prospective students were invited to a coffee klatch where they could learn about the program, meet faculty and administrators, and find out if it were possible to accomplish their objective at the institution. Local companies were called and letters were sent confirming the details. Ads were placed in the Sunday sports and Wednesday life/leisure sections of the newspaper. The Student Center Cafeteria was arranged with round tables in the center of the room, with coffee and cake set up just past the registration table. Along the walls were tables with information about the school and the program, staffed by administrators and faculty from the three departments (business, English, and psychology) who would offer degrees through the Weekend College. The program was scheduled on a Wednesday evening from 7–9 p.m. as an open house so arrival time could be flexible.

The calls began coming in on Monday morning, tapered on Tuesday, and multiplied on Wednesday. Over 75 individuals came to the open house; an additional 60 asked for information to be sent to their homes since they could not attend. For weeks after the open house, requests for information continued. The plan was to open the first program with 20 students; over 80 applied and 60 were accepted.

Another effective recruitment strategy is to showcase faculty. Invite key people from organizations to a meeting, either on campus or at a local hotel, in which a faculty member will discuss "What's Hot in _____" (business management strategies, finance, marketing, human resource management, leadership, etc.). An early morning meeting, with a continental breakfast and one-hour presentation (including questions and answers) with a brief introduction of your program as a kickoff, is most effective. Promise participants that they will be on their way by 9:45 a.m. This way they can start the day with valuable information that can be used at work that day.

Don't forget to use your alumni as marketers in an "each one, reach one" campaign. Send them a letter describing the program, why it is important, and how you need their help in marketing it. Invite them to call you about the program if they have any questions or require additional information. A few brochures should be included for them to pass on to colleagues with their name on the return form. Acknowledge the work they do by sending them a thank you for each inquiry you receive from them. Thank them for their support.

Remember—marketing is crucial to the success of the program. Conventional marketing has been undervalued by some academics and administrators, who tend to live by the "build a school and they will come" philosophy. Sound marketing strategies are most appreciated by adult and continuing educators who always need to focus on the bottom line to keep programs running. Continue to use brochures and newspaper and radio advertising. Send flyers and letters to past participants to promote a new program. Past clientele sees you as building upon previous successes. They were pleased with your services before and they'll come back to you again.

Services Designed to Serve Students

From admissions, information sources, bookstore, financial offices, computer lab and library access, parking, identification, photocopying, health and food services, to the lounge and meeting areas, cohort programs must consider a full range of services for their students. Cohort programs are designed for adults—adults who are often at work during regular work hours or are coming from work to participate in classes. Recognizing the limitations placed on their ability and willingness to run the institutional gauntlet in order to access the services or satisfy administrative requirements, cohort programs must be supported by nontraditional service providers within the institution.

Admissions

The admissions process for a cohort-based program must reflect the program philosophy. The process must be professional, simple, and complete. It should proceed in an organized manner.

In the early phases of starting a new program, the department sponsoring the program should handle all admissions office activities. The objective of most admissions departments is to generate numbers of students, whereas your objective is to recruit and retain the student who will most likely successfully complete the program. Your department is the most knowledgeable and informed about your program. So, by handling calls, correspondence, and interviews, you demonstrate to potential students and your institution that there is nothing more important than selecting the right students to comprise your first cohort.

The following processes are recommended to ensure delivery of effective and efficient student support and services.

Information Packets

Materials that are important to new students should be compiled into an information packet that is made in advance by your office and distributed to cohort program students. These packets should include:

- registration forms and course information
- financial aid forms
- book order requirements
- computer lab requirements
- library information
- parking registration forms
- food service hours and capabilities
- student health hours and available services (e.g., discount pharmacy)
- cohort lounge location and service hours

Tell students in advance that packets will be available and give them the date they must be completed. Ask them to bring their checks (for registration, books, parking), financial aid/tuition remission paperwork, and license plate numbers to the class meeting in which they will be asked to complete their packets. (After the first time they go through this process they will be familiar with it and will anticipate it and be prepared.) A memo to each student with list of required information, documentation, and payment options is very useful. Ask them to review the information so you can answer any questions immediately. Have them complete the packets and return them to you with the necessary checks, financial aid/tuition remission information, parking registration information, and book orders (with payments).

Financial Information

Financial information is very personal and private and needs to be treated as such. How a student pays for school and expenses is the student's private business. Some students have employer support for tuition and related fees. Others are paying out of pocket. Ask students if there are different payment plans that would help them to handle the expenses. Take great care to respect this phase of the process; students who receive financial aid are particularly sensitive. Financial information is given in confidence. Include the financial forms and options for methods of payment with the registration packet and process described above.

Books and Other Supplies

Include order forms in the registration packet with complete information on cost. Books can be delivered directly to the student or to your office. You can have students pick them up there during convenient hours or they can be delivered to the classroom before the course begins or during orientation. Consider having readings available by the last class meeting or prior to the new semester. Cohort students often begin reading (and faculty often expects reading and assignments prepared) before the first class meeting. Having the books available in your office brings the students there to interact with staff and feel connected to the school. This is more convenient for you and enhances the relationship between your office and the students.

Computer Lab and Library Access

This information needs to be in the registration packets, including how to activate access to both the labs and the library.

Directions to the facilities and information desks and hours should be included. Most important: include the name of someone who will be there to help them. For example, "Mary Smith staffs our computer lab from 9 a.m. to 1 p.m. and would be happy to handle your inquiries. Please call her directly at 555-5555."

Parking

If students need to register for parking, include the form and fees required in the registration packet, to be completed and returned to you along with other materials in the registration packet.

Student Identification Card

If students need identification cards, then make arrangements for the cohort group to get the identification process completed during orientation. Arrange for photos to be taken and cards created and distributed during the orientation. After the first semester, have validation stickers ready to distribute when the packets are returned completed.

Photocopy Service and Availability

Are photocopying services available? If yes, describe the service and schedule availability, fees, and time line required. Include this information, including a map with the copy machines and, if available, service areas noted on the registration packet.

Student Health Services

Although most adult students have their own physicians and health service providers, if they are paying for the service as part of their student services fee, give them the information. Let them know where the student health office is, the services provided, and the hours of availability.

Food Service

Where is the cafeteria? What hours is it available? What can you usually expect to find there at the hours the cohort is on campus? Be honest! Where are the vending machines? Are they usually stocked? You can include these locations on the map with computer lab and library locations.

Cohort Lounge/Meeting Area

Students need a place they can use as a lounge or meeting area. Include this information in the registration packet. For many cohort programs, students gather at a particular table in the cafeteria or on a special bench near the entryway of their building. The purpose is to recognize their need to be together and to give them a place to do it.

SUMMARY

This chapter discussed the cohort-based program learner. The view presented was one geared to understanding individual and group needs of students that join cohort programs. Sources of motivation with particular reference to the factors that precipitate the decision to seek a cohort-based program were considered. The interactive and self-reinforcing aspects of involvement with the cohort for learners were also addressed as well as the collaborative and intensive group learning experience provided by the cohort program. The student-focussed perspective regarding how the development of the cohort springs from programmatic and environmental structures provided a bridge to program recruitment and design. Finally, the nuts and bolts of program development and implementation with sensitivity to the cohort program learner were described. The implications of a cohort-based program and how it fits in the educational landscape will be explored in the next chapter.

CHAPTER 7

Implications for Practice

The need for educational programming that is efficient, focused, and responsive to the learning needs of adult students has never been greater. The consequences of the information age and the greater competition among world economies have created circumstances in which educational programming requires greater and greater integration with the needs of working adults and the organizations in which they work. Today's fast paced, instantly connected, complex global environment has produced and rewarded creative leaders who can "think outside the box." Consequently, the viability of educational programming is increasingly fastened to its content relevance, which must also come out of the "box." As educators have sought ways to stay ahead of these trends, different programmatic structures, especially the cohort model, have moved to the forefront.

The cohort model brings with it important features that have an impact on learners, institutions, continuing professional development, and societal implications. The need and relevance of cohort-based programming are the result of many factors that are addressed within successful programs. In examining successful cohort programs, one can identify the significance of the model for particular applications. This chapter will review some implications for practice. We will look at the impact cohorts have on society, the nature of professional education, the institutions that provide and sponsor this type of education, and the importance of internal and external networks resulting from the flourishing of cohort programs.

COHORTS AND SOCIETY

Most often, programs that are cohort-based are responding to a socially relevant need for providing a student with a particular skill set or necessary credential. These programs make a change in the greater society at large through the interaction of their subject and product, i.e., the students, with the world in which they apply their skills. The awareness of this impact is not lost on cohort program designers. On a personal level, program personnel will say, "We want to make a difference." As the ecologists put it, "Think global and act local." We have found departments and faculty working hard to create and build cohorts of learning communities within business and education throughout the United States. Is this part of the greater societal movement currently afoot to build connections among people to develop a sense of community? We think so.

Today training and education are viewed as primary vehicles to disseminate new information and cultivate a learned society. Institutional and instructional programs are specializing in certain curriculums. Undergraduate business programs have developed cohort programs in response to corporate America's emphasis on team effectiveness in the workplace. Students who learn collaborative methods of problem solving and plan implementations go back to the work environment prepared to participate in teams with experience and understanding of the team process. The emphasis on teams in the workplace has encouraged undergraduate programs, particularly those for adult reentry students, to develop cohort-based programs. Also, the business interest in cohort-based programs along with a willingness to support such programs at workplace sites has created an expanded interest in these programs.

Cohort Students

In reality, the clientele hasn't changed. Adult learners have always had and will continue to balance or juggle multiple responsibilities as they aspire to their goal of an academic credential. The societal impact that has changed is that the quality revolution in business has conditioned consumers to demand products and services that meet their needs and standards. This revolution has empowered adult learners to demand service in all venues of their lives, including education. Competition for students has forced higher education to address the needs expressed by students, particularly adult students. If there is an institution which makes the process, particularly the administrative and support processes, user friendly, the word gets out quickly and students find a way to that door. "Make the program easy to use, and they will come." Think of the book series written specifically for readers who identify themselves as "Dummies"—their primary feature is their ease of use.

The Institute for Ministry program at Loyola University, New Orleans's extension program, began about 15 years ago in response to students wanting coursework nearer to home. Today, the program can be found in over 45 Catholic dioceses, located in the United States, Canada, England, and Scotland. The program continues to grow and thrive, thus meeting the needs of pastoral ministries through collaborative initiatives.

There are more cohort-based programs on-line as the asynchronistic discussions and chat rooms engage folks to learn anywhere and anytime. If your program is not utilizing technologies, take the leap. Prospective students in your program will find you readily through search engines on the Internet. Boundaries are disappearing quickly and new linkages are being formed as we move forward in the new millennium.

COHORTS FROM
AN INSTITUTIONAL PERSPECTIVE

There are many advantages of cohort-based programs from the perspective of the institution, including the school and department, faculty, administration, and students. Cohorts can be invigorating on many levels; they can revitalize institutions intellectually and financially as well as by reputation. But, even with all of these positives, institutions should not change all of their academic programs to become cohort-based. Cohort programming is best set in a context of other educational programming. The establishment of a cohort program may attract interest from prospective students who may then elect a more traditional program of learning. Having a menu of alternative programs increases the likelihood that a prospective student will come to your institution.

Having cohort-based programs requires dramatic change within the institution. It requires commitments interfunctionally as well as intrafunctionally. Cohort-based programs must not be counter to the core values and mission of the institution if they are to be successful. These commitments and organizational matches are not possible in every institution. An institution must be committed to the group process at every level in order to serve students in cohorts successfully. Services from all departments must be coordinated because you are serving a larger number at one time. Many institutions prefer to serve a larger number on an individual basis. Neither method is better. Quality programs recognize whom they serve best and stick with it.

One of the most innovative models using the cohort structure is that employed by the Institute for Professional Development, the University of Phoenix, and the Apollo Group, Inc. Both the institute and the university are owned by the Apollo Group and represent a highly successful innovative for profit approach to adult higher education. The institute has been around for a quarter century and is a higher education development and management corporation (Sperling, 1989). Its primary work is to develop adult-oriented cohort-based programs in concert with a local college or university. Interestingly, it also provides other services to colleges like student recruitment, management training, and initial start-up capital. This investment of capital represents the institute's awareness of the primary rule of partnerships: everyone invests and everyone wins.

Collegiate Settings

Colleges and universities are providing services to students that help them to be a part of a cohort and keep them apprised of progress at the same time. For example, many colleges have web pages where applicants can check the status of their candidacy and even communicate with other prospective students. Prospective students applying to a cohort-based program can see the names and organizations of alumni on the college's web page. Some pages offer individuals the option to e-mail the alumni and ask questions directly. Colleges and universities are changing and must continuously do so to remain competitive.

Organizational Settings

Cohort programs can be housed within organizations that are not traditionally associated with learning. Innovative partnering of educators with industry where the workplace provides the platform is an increasing trend. Many corporate and non-profit organizations are sponsoring cohort groups at a workplace setting (e.g., corporation, hospital, and union). Many organizations are exploring and offering cohort-based programs to their employees or members as a service. They will give faculty meeting space including classrooms with audiovisual equipment, allow access to their employees or members, and pay a premium for this on-site option. Typically, colleges require a minimum number of students from each corporation, sometimes insisting upon a paid guarantee as part of the contractual arrangement.

One company wanted a college to sponsor a cohort program. The college guaranteed the cohort would be able to complete the entire program, graduating in 3 years. In return, the college told the company it would have to pay tuition for 15 persons whether or not there were actually 15 bodies for the duration of the program. As it turned out, all 15 students ended up graduating, but the college had covered its basic costs for delivery of this program through the contractual agreement.

Such a program has many benefits. Students don't have to travel to school. The organization can direct its employees toward a program that meets its needs. Course materials, case studies, and examples can be derived directly from the organization, and the workforce becomes more educated. That the majority of cohort-based programs have a comprehensive project or paper that learners typically base on their work is yet an added boon.

There are some disadvantages to sponsoring a cohort program at worksites. The major disadvantages are involved with the workplace relationships that exist between the students. Cross-pollination of ideas is somewhat limited because all of the students come from the same organization and share a common belief and value system. Faculty will have to work even harder to ensure that the students are challenged by new ways of thinking. When an entire cohort comes from one employer, you lose the typical diversity of students that you get when a cohort group is representative of different constituencies.

Sponsorship of cohorts is increasing. The benefits far outweigh the drawbacks for organizations and learners. For the organization, tuition and fees can be processed as a group. For learners, the camaraderie extends beyond the classroom and impacts the workplace positively as linkages develop throughout organization. Finally, when a college goes to the workplace, the market and potential for collaborative endeavors increase. Basically, your physical presence at the organization reminds them of you on a continuous basis and you become their source for everything educational.

Distance-Based Cohort Groups

Distance-based cohort groups means that there is a physical separation between the learners and the faculty person or academic institution. Nova Southeastern University in Florida is one of the better known institutions using this type of model. Nova Southeastern University uses what it calls a cluster. Similar to a cohort, a cluster is a group of students who meet together regularly with a consulting faculty person who is an expert in the field and may or may not be a faculty member at an academic institution. These meetings are accomplished with the use of technology: phone, fax, e-mail, chat rooms, and audio/video-conferencing. Students may work with other members of the group or individually, producing course work. Typically, each cluster travels to the main campus once during the semester for a real-time, in-person interaction with the group and the faculty resource person. When a group comes together for these meetings, the students often connect on several levels, depending on their interaction effectiveness during the semester. The role of the faculty resource person in creating a real cohort group cannot be overestimated. The faculty resource person must be creative and flexible with the time and space differences.

The beauty of these programs is that students come from across the country to one educational program. Students represent different regions of the United States and their coming together is representative of the melting pot America has become.

Internet

The number of programs now requiring students to have Internet access for on-line asynchronous classroom discussions and greater ease of communications is vast. Some of these programs include Thomas Edison State College's Master of Science in Management, The McGregor School of Antioch University's Master of Arts in Intercultural Relations, and the California Institute of Integral Studies. Internet usage provides a wonderful diversity of forums for communication at a distance. Colleges have replicated the campus on-line. Cohorts often have their own chat rooms, lounges, and listserves for each class. The advantage for many communicating via the Internet is how different the nature of communications is from a traditional classroom. Students can take as much time as they need to compose their thoughts before responding to someone else's comments.

Computer use has become so important that many college programs, such as the educational leadership doctoral program at the University of Sarasota in Florida, ask prospective students to include a statement of their computing skills as part of their application to the college. These programs also require Internet access as well as sufficient software skills to complete course requirements. The needs and concerns of the different constituencies involved can be met through these innovative models that have really sprung up in the last decade. On a programmatic level, you must keep thinking of new ways to communicate and more importantly keep checking that those you have continue to work.

Keep in mind that when you administer such programs from a distance, such as through the Internet, you have to be even more careful to build connections among learners, alumni, and staff. Construct student access so that communications can be observed and you can measure the interaction patterns. You may find that student interaction is so vital and exciting that staff and faculty have become tuned into e-mail communications. Be aware that you may have to supply computers and Internet access for faculty persons who will be involved with this educational endeavor. You might have to provide training as well.

NETWORKS

Cohort programs create and promote networks of people in the same profession working toward a common vision. They also generate a network of relationships between and among educators and sponsors. The relationships of the individuals that maintain these networks have an impact beyond just the success of the program. The collection of people sharing their lives in all of their classes together builds strong bonds and connections that are expressed in diverse ways.

The utility of the network to respond to the needs of the individuals and the greater social context is tied to the particular unique qualities of the cohort and the institutional and organizational context. The establishment of traditions and the connections between successive cohorts and alumni are obvious networks that can develop quickly and require only marginal support from sponsoring institutions. The sense of commonality of cohort members tends to contribute to the helpful identification with and the support of networks that emerge from the cohort experience.

The power of the cohort in developing into a cohesive force

to be reckoned with is predicated on the increasing familiarity students have with each other. They become a sort of family. Members of each cohort group are knowledgeable about each other's strengths and weaknesses and how to draw upon them to further the progress of the group. They become one and through consensus validate each other's identification with the group goals to the extent that they will sometimes act as one. This unity can challenge the institutions as a viable power base. When 20 students complain at one time about a professor; a department chair often heeds the complaint more than if only one student had voiced the same complaint. It is from this type of group experience that a continuation of networking behavior is provided even after participation in the cohort has come to an end.

Cohort groups can become incestuous and manifest all of the problems identified with inbreeding. Rather than becoming more informed and broader in scope (utilizing all of the advantages of the web network), they can become narrow and limited, focusing inward. Davis (1969) noted that cohesive groups could suffer from distracting social interaction that contributes to "reduced likelihood of successful goal attainment." It is important to remember this while working with each cohort group as a warning that there is a dark side to the cohort experience.

You will want to encourage cohort members to utilize the skills and knowledge they each bring to the group. Keep in mind one of your goals is to develop opportunities and requirements in each class for learners to access the network of each other as they create more linkages. Purposeful connections encourage individuals to stay in touch once the introductions have been made. Try to have mixers or guest speakers that revitalize the energy of your students, giving them a new purpose for networking.

PARTNERSHIPS

One of your goals ought to be to have partnerships. Partnerships are institutional relationships connected by common goals. For example, you might need assistance in resource location and allocation. Your partners may help you find them. Partners can be corporations, organizations, or other collegiate institutions. Don't pretend you won't need the assistance. You will and do. Also keep in mind that the individuals who are representatives of an institutional partner may change departments or institutions. They can then become an access point to extend your programming efforts into new areas or can otherwise provide access to resources that might help you in other ways.

Think of those who can impact program policy as partners, too. This includes administrators who represent essential areas within the institutions, department faculty, and senior administrators. They all have current information, understand the immediate issues to be addressed, and have a vested interest in the program and its success. Involving them in your process increases your credibility and influence in the organization.

Consider forming an advisory group of potential students who are alumni of your other programs. Choose representatives of corporations and organizations who might send their employees to your program. They will serve as an excellent resource for helping you to establish partnerships with organizations. Send a memo inviting them to participate in this vital committee, outline the responsibilities of the committee, and be sure to let them know how often the committee will meet and what will be expected of them. Each member of your advisory group could serve as a liaison between you and their organization.

SUMMARY

The complex global environment we live in has created a need for educational programming that integrates the needs of working adults and the organizations in which they work. The interconnectivity and instantaneous access to information have created a need for flexible, creative leaders who "push the edge of the envelope" as they anticipate and respond to the challenges of our complicated world. Cohort-based programs are an effective programming strategy designed to meet these needs as they are rooted in a collaborative model of learning and professional development. The intrinsic value of sharing ideas builds creative individuals who can meet the challenges of the 21st century.

In this chapter, we reviewed the impact of cohorts on society, the nature of professional education, and the institutions that provide and sponsor this type of education. We emphasized the importance of cohorts for the institutions that house them. Examples were taken from successful cohort-based programs from throughout the United States. We discussed the nontraditional organizations that not only house cohort programs, but also create environments where the model lives in daily organizational life. Distance-based groups and the role of the Internet were considered. Finally, networks and partnerships were discussed as individual and institutional products of effective cohort programs.

CHAPTER 8

The Future of Cohort Programming and Learning

Cohort-based programs provide organizations with opportunities to test new formats, programs, and strategies within institutions. They also function as incubators for the development of new curriculum, approaches, and policies.

The impact of these programs on institutions is considerable. The cohort model has become a compelling solution to educational needs today and as such represents one of the predominant models for serving adult learners. The majority of cohort programs undertake the intellectual as well as social development of their clientele. Expressing it most eloquently is the California Institute of Integral Studies where they "seek to express a unifying vision of humanity, world, and spirit" (Elias & Kasl, 1999, p. 5). A more commonplace description often found in the literature describing cohort programs asserts learners will spend time in interactive learning with peers, exploring issues and perspectives through rigorous intellectual inquiry. It is the attention to the pursuit of knowledge and group dynamics that conveys the future of cohort programming and learning.

COHORT PROGRAMMING: UNLIMITED POTENTIAL

Academe, like the rest of the world, is in a transformative time. Over half of the student population is over the age of 25. The average educational level of an American is increasing.

White-collar professionals and even blue-collar workers are expected to hold an undergraduate degree. It is a widely held belief that educated employees are more productive employees because they know how to think. Technology is being used to deliver instruction worldwide as well as be a communication tool for dialogue without time or location boundaries. New ways of delivering instructional programming are being created daily to meet the demands.

Within this environment, cohort programs are regarded as avant-garde because they provide entree for innovation to lead policy and program development. Often, they began as an enhancement within a particular department or, as in the case with University of Phoenix's Institute for Professional Development, as a joint venture between an organization and a college or university. They are doing well in meeting their goals. Success begets success.

The potential of the cohort model is unlimited. The connections built between individuals in pursuit of mutual goals who seek solutions together can create a better world. Transformations in education, business, or society at large can only occur when you have groups of people committed to a collective vision. That in a nutshell is the beauty of cohort programming and learning: a cadre of individuals who have learned through intensive experiential encounters how to build networks and linkages across organizational obstacles to achieve a common dream.

Employee training and development in corporate, nonprofit, and governmental sectors represent a new frontier for institutional cohort-based programs. As employee training and development are viewed as a major requirement in attracting and maintaining knowledge workers, this becomes another opportunity to employ the cohort model toward a common goal. Representatives of for profit and nonprofit organizations can work with collegiate administration and faculty or alone to develop programs that maintain, develop, and enhance the knowledge, skills, and abilities of employees as cohorts. The programs can be built around the competency-based models that are required in process-centered organizations. For example, managerial leadership programs that build skills required of leaders in the 21st century organization can be developed in partnership with organizations that require their employees to participate in programming in order to advance within the organization. The assignments and projects should be work-related projects that students have to accomplish, further strengthening the connection between the learning and application.

CREATING BETTER PROGRAMMING

Curriculum in cohort-based programming is designed so that learners have educational experiences that build on previous learning while incorporating current experiences. Because of the lockstep nature of these programs, courses build on each other, bringing learners down the pathway toward completion. The beauty here is that the end is in sight. The path is clearly delineated and marked with road stops. We can focus our efforts on the goal of creating a better tomorrow through cohort programming and learning. Faculty members of cohort-based programs are typically involved with other programming in an institution as well. Through this interaction, faculty provides a conduit for ideas that develop out of cohort programming that can be brought to traditional programs. Information gained in this way can then be used to modify other curricula. Faculty and students will be able to become quite creative as they duplicate aspects of the cohort experiences in other programs. As a beginning, we would expect to see less lectures, more group assignments, and more self-directed learning experiences as some of the adaptations that will improve educational practices everywhere. These types of strategies can easily be incorporated into course objectives so that students will take ownership of their learning experiences to move beyond traditional boundaries that may have limited their sense of involvement in the past.

As we envision the future of cohort programming and learning, the beginning of movements comes into view. The concept is still evolving. Let us begin by discussing the notion of cohorts as a community of learners.

The Cohort as a Community

Talk to those who have completed a cohort-based program and they will describe for you how everyone helped each other through the program. They are members of a community of learners. Cohort members are known for being "all for one and one for all." A cohort experience provides members with opportunities to gather information on resources, while each student serves both as a sounding board and as a resource to another. Many learners who have been members of a cohort believe that they would not have completed their program of study without the support received from other cohort learners.

These communities of learners have the power to impact national movements in professional fields. For many years, faculty from the Adult Education Guided Independent Study (AEGIS) Program of Columbia University Teachers College has held receptions for potential students, corporate representatives, alumni, and other interested parties at national conferences. This gives faculty members an opportunity to promote their conceptual framework of an international adult education movement while building connections among alumni and other interested parties on an ongoing basis. The reception has become a "place to meet and greet the elite" as the program is considered one of the premiere doctoral degree programs in adult education. As the cohort model becomes more and more commonplace, the establishment of similar groups that would interact and cross-pollinate each other is a likely next phase.

A continuing advantage of cohort-based programs is the interaction and exchange of ideas that occur after the program of study is completed. This community of learners is built upon connections between cohort members and their networks as well as faculty, administration, other cohort groups, and other professionals in the field. The relationships within the group evolve into a collegial, professional peer relationship.

As members of such a community, alumni often want to maintain their connection to the cohort, faculty, and school. As administrators of cohort-based programs we have many opportunities to maintain that connection, including inviting alumni to participate in new student orientations or seminars, to be a part of marketing initiatives as resources to new cohort groups, to participate in development opportunities, and to serve as references for potential new students. Alumni can also serve on advisory councils, combining their cohort experiences and workplace expertise to provide insights and guidance in program maintenance and growth. The cohort network provides a wonderful opportunity to keep cohort group members connected throughout the formal academic program as well as to establish lifelong ties. As the years accrue, the layers of generations of cohorts and their networks will create a chain of knowledge of process and of content. As the model endures, it will lose its novelty status and become a respected and perhaps even preferred approach to education and training.

Cohorts in the Workplace

As we look to the future, the responsive nature of the cohort-based program model and its ability to meet the needs of government concerns and industry due to its flexibility and focus leap to the forefront. Cohort programming is a perfect design for workplace training and education.

The emerging needs of organizations often focus on leadership development programs. Yet, there are many other examples of skill sets specific to a particular industry or trend that help the organization and would benefit from cohort programming and learning. For example, the pharmaceutical industry competes for life science majors who can enter the organization at entry level with knowledge of drug development and clinical trials. These processes are not taught in traditional undergraduate college programs. A cohort-based program could link the major course of study with work and study at a particular corporation to provide competencies that the pharmaceutical companies require at the entry and perhaps journeyman levels. Students would study with faculty at the collegiate institution and with scientists in the pharmaceutical industry. This would help the students to develop genuine drug development and clinical trial skills. Faculty and the scientists would work together to create a curriculum that meets the needs of the academy, the students, and industry. Collaboration between educational institutions and specific industries as equal partners creates a win-win solution for everyone involved.

The process-centered organization model, in which employees work in process teams rather than traditional functional groups (i.e., teams versus departments), provides a perfect setting for cohort-based learning. The members of the teams work together in order to accomplish goals (e.g., new drug application, new product developed). Their work requires learning strategies designed for the team in order to accomplish their goal. Organizations that develop training for these teams can utilize the cohort-based programming model quite effectively.

Members of employer-sponsored cohort groups often work better together because of the camaraderie established among them as learners. The time spent together in a learning situation creates relationships conducive to the exploration of new ways of doing things as well as focused on a particular mutual goal. Having been students together, employees leap through the initial stages of teaming because they already function and consider themselves a type of team. As industry sees the overall impact of cohort-based learning, particularly on the bottom line of productivity and worker retention, cohort programming will likely emerge as the most preferred approach to meet a variety of organizational needs.

Cohorts and Technology

We would be remiss in a chapter dealing with future trends not to discuss technology and Internet-based cohort programming. While some institutions, such as Nova Southeastern University, Thomas Edison State College, Columbia University Teachers College, and others have been using the Internet as a mode of delivery for over a decade, many other institutions are still considering the option. Think about using the cohort group process with students and faculty in a virtual environment. The sharing of ideas, design strategies, and problem solving that occurs in face-to-face interactions also occurs in other mediums of communication. The mode of contact is different, inviting learners who want and need this type of program.

Programs use teleconferencing, television broadcasting, conference calls, and other technology-based methods they have at their avail. If you are not using any of these for instruction, at a minimum consider using e-mail as a vehicle to communicate with your cohort groups. The speed of e-mail helps you be more effective in the classroom as well as in the program. Learners want to communicate with faculty, administration, and peers through a variety of options. This is just one more way to keep the channels of communication open.

The world is changing and we need to change along with it. Cohort programs are not a passing fad. They are here to stay. As technology continues to mature, there will be even greater ways of supporting the cohort's structures. The more ways we have to connect learners to each other and to instructional leaders, the more we will remain leaders in our fields. Cohort programming is ideal for connecting learners through technology-based programs. The group size is perfect for a chat room, listserve, or online classroom. We encourage you to try it. You will probably like it!

CLOSING THOUGHTS

The magic of a cohort comes from good programming that results in learning. It is the connections, the networking, and the feeling that the learners get when they know they are all on the same journey together. It is exciting for faculty and administrators to be around these learners and join them on this type of journey. We hope you will get as energized as others who have traveled down this road.

We encourage you to connect to faculty of cohort programs in other institutions in order to exchange information as well as to develop a network of colleagues who are sharing a dynamic learning experience. As much as possible, you will want a cohort of your own, consisting of members within your program and connections with others who operate other cohort programs. Modeling the core competencies of the cohort and experiencing the challenges and exhilaration of the cohort experience will enhance your ability to be effective in both cohort and traditional education environments.

The cohort programming model creates communities of learners through its supportive bonds and connections. It is very user friendly, thus it changes the faculty experience. Cohort-based programs should be viewed within the context of other program models. They will not supplant traditional programs in institutions but will instead complement them by bringing in students and resources that probably would not have come to a traditional program. These students expand the networks of administration and faculty. The specificity of cohort-based programs are, by design, limited to a precisely defined student with distinct and clear goals that cannot be met by the traditional academic program model. It is this basic tenet of the cohort-based program that will expand your organization. If you build a cohort-based program, they will come.

REFERENCES

Achilles, C. M. (1994). Searching for the golden fleece: The epic struggle continues. *Educational Administration Quarterly, 30*(1), 6–26.

Apps, J. W. (1991). *Mastering the teaching of adults.* Malabar, FL: Krieger.

Aslanian, C. B., & Brickell, H. M. (1980). *Americans in transition: Life changes as reasons for adult learning.* New York: College Entrance Examination Board.

Barnett, B. G., & Caffarella, R. S. (1992, October-November). *The use of cohorts: A powerful way for addressing issues of diversity in preparation programs.* Paper presented at the annual meeting of the University Council for Educational Administration Convention, Minneapolis, MN.

Barnett, B. G., & Muse, I. D. (1993). Cohort groups in educational administration: Promises and challenges. *Journal of School Leadership, 3,* 400–415.

Bartz, D. E., & Calabrese, R. L. (1991). Improving graduate business school programs by strengthening the delivery system. *Journal of Education for Business, 66,* 147–150.

Basom, M., Yerkes, D., Norris, C., & Barnett, B. (1995). *Exploring cohorts: Effects on principal preparation and leadership practice.* (ERIC Document Reproduction Service No. ED 387 857).

Bratlien, M. J., Genzer, S. M., Hoyle, J. R., & Oates, A.D. (1992). The professional studies doctorate: Leaders for learning. *Journal of School Leadership, 2,* 75–89.

Brookfield, S. D. (1982). Evaluation models and adult education. *Studies in Adult Education, 14,* 93–100.

Brookfield, S. D. (1986) *Understanding and facilitating adult learning: A comprehensive analysis of principles and effective practices.* San Francisco: Jossey-Bass.

Brookfield, S. D. (1990) *The skillful teacher: On technique, trust, and responsiveness in the classroom.* San Francisco: Jossey-Bass.

Cambron-McCabe, N., Mulkeen, T. A., & Wright, G. K. (1991). *The Danforth program for professors of school administration: A new platform for preparing school administrators.* Saint Louis: The Danforth Foundation.

Candy, P. C. (1991). *Self-direction for lifelong learning: A comprehensive guide to theory and practice.* San Francisco: Jossey-Bass.

Chene, A. (1983). The concept of autonomy in adult education: A philosophical discussion. *Adult Education Quarterly, 34* (11), 38–47.

Cohen, N. H. (1995). *Mentoring adult learners.* Malabar, FL: Krieger.

Cross, K. P. (1981). *Adults as learners: Increasing participation and facilitating learning.* San Francisco: Jossey-Bass.

Darkenwald, G. G., & Merriam, S. B. (1982). *Adult education: Foundations of practice.* New York: Harper & Row.

Davis, J. H. (1969). *Group performance.* Reading, MA.: Addison-Wesley.

Davies, T. G. (1997, May). Blending learning modalities: A return to the "high tech/high touch" concept. (www.thejournal.com)

Elias, J., & Kasl, E. (1999). California Institute of Integral Studies. [Brochure]. San Francisco: CA.

Galbraith, M. W. (1998). *Adult learning methods* (2nd ed.). Malabar, FL: Krieger.

Giles, F. (1983, March). *The effects of doctoral study on marriage and family: An ethnographic study.* Paper presented at the annual meeting of the American College Personnel Association, Houston, TX.

Hiemstra, R., & Sisco, B. (1990) *Individualizing instruction: Making learning personal, empowering, and successful.* San Francisco: Jossey-Bass.

Institute for Professional Development. (1997). *Institute for Professional Development: Building on a tradition of innovation* [Brochure]. Phoenix, AZ: IPD.

Johnson, D. W., & Johnson, F. P. (1987) *Joining together: Group therapy and group skills.* Englewood Cliffs, NJ: Prentice-Hall.

Kasworm, C. E., & Blowers, S. S. (1994). *Adult undergraduate students: Patterns of learning involvement* (Contract no. R117E10015). Knoxville: The University of Tennessee, College of Education.

Knowles, M. S. (1980). *The modern practice of adult education: From pedagogy to androgogy.* (Rev. ed.). Chicago: Association Press.

Knowles, M. S. (1984). (1975) *Self-directed learning: A guide for learners and teachers.* Chicago: Association Press.

Knowles, M. S. (1984). "Introduction: The art and science of helping adults learn." In M. S. Knowles and Associates, *Androgogy in ac-*

tion: Applying modern principles of adult learning. San Francisco: Jossey-Bass.

Landa, A., & Tarule, J. (1992) *Models of collaboration in postsecondary education II.* The Collaborative Learning Project of the Lesley College Center for Research, Pedagogical and Policy Studies. Cambridge, MA.

Long, H. (1983). *Adult learning: Research and practice.* New York: Cambridge Books.

Loyola University. (1997). *Loyola Institute for Ministry extension program prospectus.* [Brochure]. New Orleans: Loyola University New Orleans Institute for Ministry.

Luikart, C. (1977). Social networks and self-planned adult learning (Doctoral dissertation, The University of North Carolina at Chapel Hill, 1976). *Dissertation Abstracts International, 77,* 2072.

Maguire, L. (1983). *Understanding social networks.* Beverly Hills, CA: Sage.

Malaney, G. D. (1987, November). *A decade of research on graduate students: A review of the literature in academic journals.* Paper presented at the Association for the Study of Higher Education, Baltimore, MD.

Mezirow, J. (1990) *Transformative dimensions of adult learning.* San Francisco: Jossey-Bass.

Milstein, M. M., & Associates, (1993). *Changing the way we prepare educational leaders: The Danforth experience.* Newbury Park, CA: Sage.

National Commission on Excellence in Education. (1983). *A nation at risk: The imperative for educational reform.* Washington, DC: U.S. Government Printing Office.

National-Louis University. (1995). *National-Louis University Ed. D. in adult education prospectus.* [Brochure]. Chicago: National-Louis University.

Pascarelli, E. T., & Terenzini, P. T. (1991). *How college affects students: Findings and insights from twenty years of research.* San Francisco: Jossey-Bass.

Reynolds, K. C., & Hebert, F. T. (1995). Cohorts, formats and intensive schedules: Added involvement and interaction for continuing higher education. *The Journal of Continuing Higher Education, 43*(3), 34–42.

Russo, C. S. (1996). Speech, Professional Development Program. *Association for Continuing Higher Education,* Spring, 1996. Rutgers University, Newark, N.J.

Saltiel, I. (1994). *Support systems: A comparison of factors that influence adult doctoral and undergraduate students who are employed full time.* Unpublished doctoral dissertation, Fordham University, New York.

Schmuck, P. A. (1988). *Preparing superintendents for the unexpected, the unanticipated and the untoward.* (ERIC Document Reproduction Service No. ED 309 548)

Smith, B. L. (1993). Creating learning communities. *Liberal Education, 79*(4), 32–39.

Smith, R. M. (1982). *Learning how to learn: Applied learning theory for adults.* New York: Cambridge Books.

Sperling, J. G. (1989). *Against all odds.* Phoenix, AZ: Apollo Press.

Tarr-Whelan, L., (1987, October). *Preparing America's workforce.* Center for Policy Alternatives: Washington, DC.

University of Phoenix. (1998). *University of Phoenix online campus degree programs in business, management, and technology* [Brochure]. Phoenix, AZ: Author.

Weise, K. R. (1992, October). *Through the lens of human resource development: A fresh look at professional preparation programs.* Paper presented at the annual meeting of the University Council for Educational Administration (Minneapolis, MN). ED 355 667.

Yerkes, D. M., Basom, M. R., Norris, C., & Barnett, B. (1995, August). *Using cohorts in the development of educational leaders.* Paper presented at the Annual International Conference of the Association of Management (Vancouver, British Columbia, Canada,). ED 387 858.

Yerkes, D., Norris, C., Basom, P., & Barnett, B. (1994). Exploring cohorts: Effects on principal preparation and leadership practice. *Connections! Conversations on Issues of Principal Preparation, 2* (3), 1, 5–8.

Zander, A. (1994). *Making groups effective* (2nd ed.). San Francisco: Jossey-Bass.

INDEX